leadership

AN EAGLE-EYE PERSPECTIVE

Help for failing leaders all over the world and for those
who want to mature their leadership gift

OGHENETHOJA UMUTEME

leadership

AN EAGLE-EYE PERSPECTIVE

MEMOIRS

Cirencester

Published by Memoirs

MEMOIRS
PUBLISHING

Memoirs Books

25 Market Place, Cirencester, Gloucestershire, GL7 2NX
info@memoirsbooks.co.uk www.memoirspublishing.com

(c) Oghenethoja Umuteme, August 2012
First published in England, August 2012
Book jacket design Ray Lipscombe

ISBN 978-1-909304-02-4

Unless otherwise indicated, Bible quotations are taken from the King James Version and New King James Version of the Holy Bible. Scripture quotations marked NIV are taken from the Holy Bible, New International Version, copyright 1973, 1978, 1984 by the International Bible Society.

Address all enquiries to the publisher;
Restoration Media House Limited +234-8092496045, +2348076190064,
Email: rmhltd.info@gmail.com

Although the author and publisher have made every effort to ensure that the information in this book was correct when going to press, we do not assume and hereby disclaim any liability to any party for any loss, damage, or disruption caused by errors or omissions, whether such errors or omissions result from negligence, accident, or any other cause. The views expressed in this book are purely the author's.

Printed in England

To my mentor, and the most reliable teacher on earth: the Holy Spirit of God, who taught me leadership. And to my parents, Elder Umuteme Moses Eboh and Mrs. Umuteme Florence, who never spared the rod when I erred as a growing child.

leadership

AN EAGLE-EYE PERSPECTIVE

CONTENTS

INTRODUCTION

1-2-3-4-5, 1-2-3-4-5... the clock in my sitting room went on and on. I was gazing at the elegant second hand, which has to count 1-2-3-4-5 repeatedly 12 times before the minute hand moves. Then the minute hand will repeat this same cycle before the hour hand moves a step further. And as they relate together in this stepwise duty call, the day gently gives way to the night.

One day I came home to discover that the beautiful second hand was still, and as long as it did not move, the minute hand and the hour hands did not move either. I got the clock and changed the battery, and, as if waving goodbye, it started off its job again.

As I lay on my bed that night, I imagined what the world would become if we could all just function like the second hand of the clock, which painstakingly and routinely does its job without complaint. And for every cycle it runs, it gives a helping hand to our plans and aspirations in life.

To me, that second hand demonstrates what the beauty of leadership is all about. It shows that leadership is about going through a cyclical process of beautification, and for every cycle, we ought to add value to the life of somebody.

I also know that when leaders become stale in performance, they need to be energised, the way the battery energised the clock, to keep going. And just as I had to set the time to the current time, all failing leaders need to be helped to recover all the time and opportunities they might have lost when they were not performing.

This learning from the clock hands made me understand better what God called me to do. He had said to me, 'I have called you to raise leaders who will execute my will on earth'. What the second hand was doing was raising the minute hand one step further every time it completed that cycle of twelve fives.

Looking at our leadership characters and work cycles, can we say we have added value to the world God put into our care? Adam was to tender the garden, until sin took him out. Moses was to take the children of Israel into a land flowing with milk and honey, until his anger took him out. Solomon was the man the world sought after, until his heart took him out.

What are we saying? Should we avoid becoming leaders because the challenges of leading others are like the second hand of the clock?

To me, the three hands of the clock represent the growth level in leadership qualities development. The hour hand represents the new recruits, or those who have to undergo the new believers' class in the church, for instance. The minute hand is the disciples, and the second hand represents the leader. The second hand has to move from the 12 o'clock position to the 6 o'clock position and back again to 12, to ensure the minute hand moves one step forward. The minute hand moves in like manner to make the hour hand move forward one step. And the hour hand moves in like manner to represent the perfect order of God, the creation of day and night, seasons and time.

The second hand works more than the minute hand and the minute hand works more than the hour hand. This is the perfect order of the sharing of leadership responsibilities. The leader spends all the night thinking and planning, as it relates to the vision he is driving, and what will be executed the following day by those he leads.

If the hands of the clock are not properly aligned, though the synchronised motion will still happen, the time representation will be affected, and everyone who looks at the clock will be misinformed about the time of the day. This minute negligence could affect the lives, fortunes, relationships, progress etc of those who depend on the timing of the clock. This also happens when there is disagreement between leaders, their disciples and those general followers; once there is misalignment in their roles and responsibilities, and misrepresentation of vision, the general public are led astray. This is the reason why those who look up to Satan are led astray, because Satan has never been in a good relationship with God, and because of his misaligned nature he can only give misaligned information to his subscribers.

As leaders we have to work round the clock, enduring the ups and downs we go through to grow. Those who are afraid of disappointments can never lead successfully. This is the lesson of the hands of the clock.

As we watch the clock hands turn again, I want to explain briefly here that leadership is lordship, and one can only lead successfully when empowered with the spirit of the Lord, who is the Holy Spirit. He is the beauty of leadership. Without Him, the disciples were mere empty vessels who were locking themselves away from being intimidated by the Jewish authorities. Even as you experience the worst situation in your life, and feel intimidated by consistent failures and disappointments, I call you to accept the Holy Spirit, and you will be bold enough to tranquillize that timid Satan, the old serpent, who roars around, all in an attempt to mock you.

This book is the outcome of leadership experience and observation and the inspiration I received from the Holy Spirit, from primary school through to secondary school, where I was the class prefect, and in the university while studying, where I had to hold some leadership positions. My industry experience of procurement supervision, job planning and engineering works supervision also served as background knowledge as I wrote this book.

Through observation, I have come to see leadership in various perspectives – from my childhood as I learned from my parents, watching school administrators leading the school system while in school, reading about leadership successes and failures in journals and watching leadership debates on TV. Taking up the leadership role in a church is not an easy obligation, as one has to depend on the Holy Spirit. This is where my inspiration judgement is coming from, which actually made this book a unique teaching on the subject of leadership.

Complex as a spiritual leadership calling may seem, it has been my joy that through the 19th day of October 2008, when I became a Pastor called by God, to the moment at which I write this final line of the introduction to this book, the 28th day of June 2012, the Holy Spirit has been there speaking behind me, giving me guidance on how to lead the children of God. In 2009, the Lord laid it in my heart to commence a leadership academy – Umuteme Leadership Academy (ULA) - and I was wondering how to start. This book has proven that the Lord is equipping me to take up the task of raising God-loving leaders for Him, who would take up the mantle of leadership wherever they may function with the fear of God live in their hearts.

This book will provide help for failing leaders all over the world and for those who want to mature their leadership gift. It contains information as part of the trainings God is taking me through, so that I will not fail. I encourage you to read it with an open mind and you will see the leadership beauty the book has to offer. Shalom!

Pst. Oghenethoja Umuteme
President/Founder
Royal Diamonds Int'l Church
(Christ Movement)
Port Harcourt, Nigeria.

CHAPTER ONE

THE ESSENCE OF LEADERSHIP

The word 'essence', within this context, is used to explain the core values of leadership, or the fundamental attributes of who a leader is. The problem we have today is that we have too many bosses in our workplaces and even in the church, instead of leaders. A boss is someone who says 'Go and do it', while a leader is one who says 'let us go and do it'. A leader is fundamentally involved in the work process, working as a visionary, planner, watchman and executor. The purpose of the Holy Spirit in our lives is to turn us into fundamental leaders who do the will of God on earth.

I have decided to start this book with this topic so as to provoke the intellectual instinct of the reader into appreciating the quintessence of the mystery behind leadership. The husband says he is the head of the family. His wife feels uncomfortable when milk is spilled and waits hopelessly for the expected head to take charge, only to discover that he is a 'headless head'. She has to clean it up herself.

Many of us claim to be elders, the question is: how 'elder' are we in that 'eldership' position? Elderliness comes with experience, not the presence of grey hairs. Leviticus 19:32 says that we must honour the man with the grey hair, what is referred to here is elderly wisdom, which comes with age. However, this is not the case with this present generation, who have neglected God's wisdom. This is one of the reasons for this discourse – we are lacking leaders all over the world.

A child says he/she is the eldest in the house and therefore has the answer the younger ones questions. Then all hell is let loose when he/she proves to barely know what to do when answers are most needed.

In school the most intelligent feels above everyone else, and lecturers look up to him/her to have a clue as to what the subject is all about. Then bolts are loosed when he/she fails an examination. I could go on and on. As you read this, you will also ask yourself if you are really a leader who finds a way when none is obvious.

Our example remains God, who created a wonderful world out of chaos. Genesis 1:1 says the earth was without form. God brought form into a formless world because it was His desire to make the world a place to be inhabited. Form means orderliness.

Man lost these attributes of leadership when Adam sinned against God. I will blame only Adam for what happened in Genesis 3, because Adam never reflected the 'watchman' characteristic of dynamic leaders. Noah slept and he became naked. Adam disobeyed God and he became naked. Saul disobeyed God when he failed to stopped his soldiers from disobeying God (1 Samuel 15:22). Leadership nakedness is borne out of lack of purpose and focus. When leaders lose their grip on what they are supposed to do because they have lost visionary consciousness, they become naked and are readily thrown into shame (Jeremiah 8:9). In the book of Hosea 4:7; the people sinned against God, because as they were increasing in size, demands, knowledge, intelligence, awareness, largeness of heart etc, they could not have a leader who could lead them rightly before God. This could be seen in the book of Ezekiel 34, where all the shepherds went astray.

Doing the right thing at the right time through the right process is what sustains our destiny. Destiny is, therefore, not about dreams and/or fictions, but discovering the unknown through the known. Jesus said that the fruit on a tree is enough evidence to know what the tree is capable of (Matthew 7:16).

Your destiny is tied to your present expectations and experiences. Employers of labour usually demand CVs from job applicants so that they can know their employees' capacity and growth potential. The interviews conducted for prospective employees provide enough evidence to have an idea about the workability culture or expectations of the intending staff.

THE HOLY SPIRIT AND LEADERSHIP

The spirit of the Lord (Isaiah 11:2) is the spirit of leadership. It is the spirit of lordship, and the power to confront disappointments. In 1 Peter 3:12, He is referred to as the spirit of righteousness. He is the spirit of authority (Acts 1:8), and the spirit of Christ (Galatians 4:4-6), the power and wisdom of God in action (1 Corinthians 1:24) and the one that proceeds from God the father (John 15:26). We all know that God is a leader, who led His children with the pillar of fire and the cloud (Exodus 13:21-22). He is a God of order (Isaiah 9:6-7), and requires that His children be led in a simple leadership framework that encompasses His character and wellbeing.

When we are out of tune with God, can we ever lead effectively? Jesus taught us that greatness is a reward for service (Matthew 23:11). I will define a leader in simple terms as 'a humble follower who gave up all he/she ever had for the purpose of establishing a bond of relationship between God and man'.

To lead others, we must submit to the leadership authority of God. This is because we are all elemental creations of God by origin (Psalms 148:1-5), and by that singular standard of being God's image and likeness, we ought to submit ourselves to Him so that the Holy Spirit can direct our path (Proverbs 3:6).

THE WORKS OF LEADERSHIP

We are going to have a walk with the ultimate leader Himself, the Lord Jesus, so that we can understand the works of leadership. When leadership is at work, failure, laziness, incompetence, subjugation, disapprovals, occupational malice, differential redundancy, etc, are often absent. This is because, before they can raise their ugly heads to disrupt the work process, the dynamic and spirit-filled leader is already aware of them, and they are rendered passive (Isaiah 42:9). Once they are out of the way, you will not fail in your drive to achieve your targets.

The Bible is evidential in feeding us with facts that are not only real, but undoubted secrets in effective leadership. For example:

- Jesus washed the feet of His disciples to demonstrate humility in service.
- He gave thanks to God before breaking bread to demonstrate appreciation and accountability.
- He associated with sinners to prove to them that theirs is the kingdom of God, if only they can repent.
- He handed over His mother to John and vice versa, to demonstrate accountability.
- He made a new friend even at the point of death, and that friend is one of those He was dying for.

- He forgave whole-heartedly when he said 'father forgive them...'
- At death He released those who were held captive and set them free.
- At resurrection, He taught His disciples more kingdom secrets and fellowshipped with them, demonstrating focus on vision and purpose.
- Before He ascended into Heaven, He made a promise of sending down a comforter (John 14:23), because He had earlier promised them not to leave them as orphans (John 14:18). This demonstrates leadership comfort in a chaotic situation, just as God did in Genesis 1:1-2 when God rescued the world from deadness.
- At the point of ascension He taught His disciples the purpose of the Holy Spirit once more, demonstrating leadership focus.
- On getting to the father, the promise was fulfilled (Acts 2), demonstrating leadership integrity.

Leadership is all about problem solving. I always tell my congregation that Christians are problem solvers and not complainers. We have too many fault finders hopelessly poisoning the minds of those who would have been serving leaders both in the church and society.

LEADERSHIP IN A HOPELESS SITUATION

The true test of leadership is when the ship is heading for destruction. An iceberg is ahead, but the rudder seems unable to turn the ship. This is when the experience of the captain is put to the test. In the parting of the Red Sea by Moses, God lighted the darkness in the desert through His pillar of fire. Moses' inexperience at the onset would have restricted his ability to deal with the situation, but his ears were alert to hear the wisdom of direction from God.

Peter's inexperience also at the beginning would have made everyone feel he was unqualified to be one who would do exploits for the Kingdom – he even decided to take the disciples back to the sea to fish after the death of Jesus, but with Jesus and the right counselling Peter would be seen confronting his fears (Acts 2). Jonah's hiding away in the ship when there was chaos while others were busy trying to rescue the ship is not leadership, but his volunteering to step out of the ship into the waters, knowing that he was the cause of the uproar at sea, is leadership. Jesus calmed the sea to ensure the boat would not capsize – this again is leadership.

What about Paul in Acts 27 - how did he help the crew and passengers aboard the ship to sail to shore? 'And as the shipmen were about to flee out of the ship, when they had let down the boat into the sea, under colour as though they would have cast anchors out of the foreship, Paul said to the centurion and to the soldiers, Except these abide in the ship, ye cannot be saved' – Acts 27:30-31. Here everybody looked up to the captain, but the dynamic leadership spirit in Paul saved them all from death.

This is leadership in action. Eve was silent, even when Adam blamed her solely for all that befell them. Again this is a demonstration of maturity in leadership. To me Eve was the real leader, not Adam. The Bible says she gave to her husband, who was right there with her, and Adam couldn't resist the temptation, showing that Adam was rather a frail leader. Mary, the mother of Jesus, knowing that the wedding celebrants needed wine, told the disciples of Jesus to do whatever He said (John 2:5) - this also is leadership. Without it the marriage ceremony would have been in jeopardy, but she saved the situation.

There is a peculiar situation which was in need of leadership in Genesis 1:1. The earth was without form, there was absolute chaos and the best way to describe the situation is the existence of 'nothingness'. What we are going to learn here points to creativity and problem solving.

We can judge it this way; God created heaven and earth, only to discover that the earth was without form, of no use and certainly of no value. He knew that the reason heaven was not experiencing the chaos the earth was seeing was because of His presence, so He sent the Holy Spirit, thereby making the earth His footstool.

A leader encounters this kind of situation daily, coming into contact with valueless situations. Even without absolute value in the forefront, leaders must always endeavour to solve the problems before them; this is what makes a leader 'tick'. We can always learn from God, who started off by sending His Holy Spirit.

This was His thinking and heartfelt wish. He wished to have a creation which was perfect and well pleasing. That wish travelled through the poles of the new earth and the dimensions of the new heaven. The Holy Spirit's mandate was to investigate the scope and analyse what was needed to take God's universal heartfelt wish for the embryonic earth off His heart, so as to get value out of nothingness.

So, as leaders, once faced with this kind of situation, all we need do is to get value out of nothingness. Every disadvantage is an avenue for exploring the leadership potential lying fallow in us. This is what I refer to often as 'treasure in disguise'.

In the book of Romans 4:18-24, we are told that Abraham's old age never bothered him as he waited to see the vision ahead of him come through. By this singular act it was imputed to him for righteousness, which in this sense means right standing with God. Righteousness is leadership, because anyone who is standing right with God is always favoured by God, and anyone favoured by God is led by God. Every one led by God is himself a leader.

THE SENSE OF LEADERSHIP

We are all aware of the five senses that coordinate all we do in life. Leadership sensitivity (LS) is intelligent enquiry into the issues that matter at that moment in time. It is a product of spiritual sensitivity and physical sensitivity. Jesus knew the minds of His disciples and of those who confronted Him daily. Leadership sensitivity helps us in providing answers that adequately meet the needs of the immediate situation and provide clues into the future, both in the physical and in the spiritual.

Spiritual sensitivity allows you to see behind the scenes, as many things we see do not appear to be what they are. More than 80% of the volume of an iceberg is submerged beneath the surface of the sea. Physical sensitivity is actually borne out of experience. Moses was spiritually sensitive, though he had little physical experience of leading a nation at the heart of God to Him; he was able to connect to the spirit realm to bring them the Ten Commandments.

A leader sits down to think, pray, meditate and seek God's spirit of wisdom, spirit of knowledge, of understanding and of counsel, and of the fear of the Lord, and of strength (Isaiah 11:2). These are the embodiment of leadership sense.

CREATIVE LEADERSHIP

Leadership is about problem solving, and so is creativity. The book of Genesis 1:3 opened our understanding to the creative power of God. In this verse, God created illumination, which is the value of problem solving. And the result shows that only a portion of that nothingness received light, and the remaining portion remained in darkness. So He separated the darkness from the light.

Always know your success and separate it from the disappointments that come your way, which is why we also sing 'count your blessings and name them one by one.' Learn to always count your chickens once they are hatched, and know your unhatched eggs. This also helps you to know where to make savings. A creative leader must be able to separate odd encounters from the productive results. Here, the light of God must shine on us. In Exodus 31:1-3, we learn that creativity is only possible with the Spirit of God: Wisdom, Knowledge and Understanding.

THE HEART OF LEADERSHIP

In that same Genesis chapter 1 verse 3, we can elucidate more on the resulting light and darkness that evolved as God's Holy Spirit hovered through the depth of that primitive creation that received the attention of God. And in our leadership perspective, seeing light in our investments means we are having elements of motivation, encouragement, help, increased opportunities to excel, and the like. Darkness on the other hand could mean disappointments, mockers, excessive customer complaints etc.

When the Holy Spirit moved, there was an incubation process, and that process only turned a fraction of the void into light. God never mentioned darkness when He said, 'let there be' because 'void' is the same as darkness so darkness already existed, but He got light from it.

Now in my deepest thoughts, I have reasoned that there was actually coldness and unfriendliness all over the earth because there was no sun yet. The light God created in verse 3 is not the sun but spiritual illumination, or what I will call creative abilities or advantages. In my book *How good and large is your land?* I defined disability as the inability to see your abilities. So God could be said to have turned a fraction of the disabled creation, which was without form, a kind of gaseous mass floating on the water surface, into streams of abilities. This is what I call goodness coming out of darkness. And Samson called it food coming out of the eater.

So the heart of every leader is to create goodness out of chaos, which is also the reason you are a Christian. This is the message I want to pass across in this opening chapter; that leaders are out to solve problems, and with the help of God's Holy Spirit, we can turn darkness into light.

LEADERSHIP TOOL

The image you envision and bear in your mind is what grows inside you and makes you who you are. The Holy Spirit of God is the only leadership tool we need, because this is God's gift of leadership to us (Genesis 2:7); He is the one who proceeds from the Father and has understood the earth from creation, making Him one filled with enormous wisdom and knowledge about the earth. And this tool is a person, who must be the chief executive of the adventure you are about to embark on.

Jesus said in John 15:5 that without Him we cannot do anything. And in Acts 1:8, He gave us the final hope of things to come, which can only come through faith (Hebrew 11:6). Jeremiah explained this when He said that those who put their trust in God will always experience freshness through and through (Jeremiah 17:7-9). Once we are established through the help of the Holy Spirit, we become leaders who move mountains.

With the Holy Spirit feeding us the wisdom, knowledge and understanding of God, we would be able to recruit the right people to work with us so that we would succeed. Gideon had 32,000 soldiers instead of 300. God's intervention in his case proved that leaders must rely on Him in order not to waste resources (Judges 7). What baffles me was how he was able to convince so many soldiers. When he told the other 31,700 to go back, they didn't even quarrel and cause pandemonium in his camp. This is because the hand of God was with him.

LEADERSHIP CHOICE

Leadership is about making the right choice. Those who consistently make mistakes are not leaders. Jesus was led into the wilderness by the Holy Spirit for a tempting adventure, but when the tempter did came, He resisted him, and that success gave Him the right perspective to choose His disciples, whom He said God gave Him (John 15:16, John 17:6).

As you read further, pray that God should order your footsteps, so that you will always be able to make the right choice of those who will stand to work with you and take the right decision, all the time. Many leaders have made mistakes due to the choices they make daily which now affect their leadership styles, which would have been productive.

CHAPTER TWO

LEADERSHIP TENETS

A tenet is defined as an opinion, doctrine or principle held as being true by a person or especially by an organization. How will a woman know, for instance, if her husband is a leader? As I said earlier, and I want to emphasis here again, the man normally says 'I am the head of the house, how functional is the head?' The wife will say, 'In this house I am supposed to know what is happening.' Are you a casual wife - because a wife is also a leader - so you won't know what is happening?

Leadership tenets are the doctrinal emphasis of what leadership entails. We have talked about the essence of leadership, which deals with the main core values of leadership and its bearers, who we now call leaders. There we made mention of leadership attributes, and concerns of our Lord and Saviour, Jesus Christ on leadership through His exemplary life while on earth.

We shall be discussing these tenets from first principles. We all know that God is the origin of all things, because He first existed and then caused other things to exist, and these things are the reason He created man to tender His garden at Eden. We are still growing in our knowledge of leadership, and we need to walk into the leadership environment in this discussion.

Leadership is stewardship. No one can claim to be a child of God when they cannot come out to put things right in their homes, neighbourhoods and larger society. Since leadership starts and ends with God, because He is the author and finisher of our lives, we can't claim to love God when we find it difficult to do the work He wants us to do. The Bible says we should all be found steadfastly working where we had been assigned by the Holy Spirit of God. Inasmuch as God is our ultimate leader who leads us with a voice speaking from behind us to guide us through the path of righteousness (Isaiah 30:21, Isaiah 42:19), we should not try to freeze the word of God in the morgue if we are truly Christians. This word is the beginning of leadership.

Nobody can stop the work of God, so we either evangelize or stay out of it. Now evangelism traits in us will enable politicians to make better, God-fearing manifestos. The same goes to anybody taking an oath of office, who should be careful with swearing by the Bible, knowing that he/she will not rule outside its provisions.

Even in the law courts, those who take oath under the

pretence of upholding the truth will be careful to do so if they are evangelists. This implies that if we are to borrow a leaf from Jesus, who commenced His leadership with evangelism, we would expect that every God-fearing leader should first engage his/her self with the work of evangelism. This is because the act of evangelism is the act of reaching out. Leadership involves giving people information.

Do you know what it takes to be the head of the house? It starts with God. He told the Israelites 'what you are giving me; give it to your governor whether they will accept your person' – Malachi 1:8. Leadership is what keeps you on an authority that makes you have that control over people's knowledge and anger, lead your children rightly and set a standard for others to follow. That's what makes someone a leader.

THE PAINS OF HAVING NO LEADERSHIP

The children of Israel, because of their disobedience to God, after they had left the land of Egypt through the strong hand of God, were now suffering. Because they were suffering, they needed to come out of their bondage through a permanent solution. God had given them leaders - judges, kings and prophets - but none was able to take them out of pain, none could give them peace, so there was a climax of suffering. In Isaiah 1:3-4 God spoke with indignation about how the children of Israel had honoured Him:

The ox knoweth his owner, and the ass his master's crib: but Israel doth not know, my people doth not consider. Ah sinful nation, a people laden with iniquity, a seed of evildoers, children that are corrupters: they have forsaken the Lord, they have provoked the Holy One of Israel unto anger, they are gone away backward.

They did not know their leader. The people were languishing in pain, and Jeremiah came to prophesy the heart of God to them at one time, in Jeremiah 17:9-10, showing that the pains they were experiencing were borne out of the fact that they had neglected the ultimate leader Himself – Yahweh. In whatever we do, we are going to have a reward. The children of Israel were reaping what they sowed. Wherever we are and in everything we do we are leaders, as long as we are exercising the gift in us.

There is an action life or character people expect us to put on as leaders, but when these are not showing, we end up leading people astray, and because we've led them astray, they will harvest strangeness unto us, giving us what we've sown into their lives. Now if we read down to Isaiah Chapter 1 verses 16-17, we would see that the absence of leadership is very evident as the people didn't know what to do:

Wash yourselves, make yourselves clean; put away the evil of your doings from before mine eyes; cease to do evil; Learn to do well; seek judgment, relieve the oppressed, judge the fatherless, plead for the widow.

We can see the tenets coming out clearly in this portion of the Bible: cleanliness, putting away evil, learning to do well, seeking judgement, relieving the oppressed, judging the fatherless and pleading for the widow. Our ability to do all these will definitely reduce the chaos in society, as there will be orderliness. To do all these, the leaders must have a documented process in place, where who handles what is outlined. If you sow goodness into somebody's life the person will be the better for it, but when you are unable to change that person to become good, you discover at the end of the day that you end up losing the goodness that would have come through that person. So, we could say that the pain of the absence of leadership is chaos and lack of vision. Leadership drives vision.

Implying that when we touch lives one by one and let those lives we touch also, in like manner, touch other lives, leadership will come into place whereby everybody will have access to the principles of life; wisdom, knowledge and understanding. Without genuine leadership in place, these essences of life will be missing.

The problem many of us are having today is that since we are not able to sow goodness, we are also unable to reap it, and the same thing goes to our lukewarm attitudes towards evangelism. When you sow into the hearts of people, you will see them responding to what you are doing. This was how

Gideon recruited the 32,000 soldiers who followed him to war. But not until we sow the principles of leadership into the hearts of people, will we be sleeping behind burglar-proof doors. Our inability to sow righteousness into the hearts of people is the reason behind the ills in society today. The question now is - who will sow this seed of righteousness?

LEADERSHIP IS SOWING

There is a difference between a son and a child. God gave us the understanding to our problems when he said a child would be born, and that child was not going to be an ordinary child but a son, and that the government would be upon His shoulder (Isaiah 9:6). 'And there will be a spirit upon that son, and he will work zealously for God.' For without zeal, He would not achieve. This is the sowing spirit in every leader. Zeal has to do with something that burns in your heart. If you are zealous for the work of God, at the end of the day you will know what to do to ensure you walk with Him perfectly. And as you walk with Him, your leadership attributes and character will begin to bear fruit. This is why in John 15:5 Jesus said that without Him we can do nothing, because we have to apply the wisdom He has taught while on earth, which the Holy Spirit will bring to our remembrance.

THE DOCTRINE OF LEADERSHIP

What we need to derive from this is the need to grow into responsible leaders. Jesus says we must learn of Him after we have given Him our burden (Matthew 11:28). A leader is somebody who is responsible and lives by example. When you have enough leaders in the house, you will discover that things will work normally. In the church we have the doctrine of trinity, God the Father, Son and Holy Spirit. We have another doctrine in the church and society, that a woman should respect her husband. We have the doctrine that children should be submissive to their parents, elders, and rulers, etc. To understand what leadership entails, I want us to understand the terms of redemption contained in Isaiah 9:6-7:

For unto us a child is born, unto us a son is given: and the government shall be upon his shoulder: and his name shall be called Wonderful, Counsellor, The mighty God, The everlasting Father, The Prince of Peace. Of the increase of his government and peace there shall be no end, upon the throne of David, and upon his kingdom, to order it, and to establish it with judgment and with justice from henceforth even forever. The zeal of the LORD of hosts will perform this.

To me, this is the leadership doctrine, which is also the doctrine of government, and leaders all over the world must pursue it to become established. From these two verses we find the major duties of a leader. The child must grow to become a son. That is how leadership skill grows in us. The Bible says in Luke 2:40, 52: 'And the child grew, and waxed strong in spirit, filled with wisdom: and the grace of God was upon him. And Jesus increased in wisdom and stature, and in favour with God and man'.

We become mature and well nurtured over the years when we know that we are placed in a position to bring God's ultimate redemption plan into reality. These duties have also become doctrines of truth. We all know that the truth sets us free, and Jesus is the prince of peace, which means that in Jesus we receive our own leadership spirit, to speak the truth and also to hear the truth. He is the power of God and the wisdom of God, which becomes that voice that leads us out of chaos, saying: 'this is the way, walk ye in it' –Isaiah 30:21. In Isaiah 55:3, hearing is seen as an ingredient of leadership: 'Incline your ear, and come unto me: hear, and your soul shall live...' We must hear, and observe before we can respond to people's complaints as leaders. Here is what the prophet Isaiah said about Jesus:

He is despised and rejected of men; a man of sorrows, and acquainted with grief: and we hid as it were our faces from him; he was despised, and we esteemed him not. Surely he hath borne our griefs, and carried our sorrows: yet we did esteem him stricken, smitten of God, and afflicted. But he was wounded for our transgressions, he was bruised for our iniquities: the chastisement

of our peace was upon him; and with his stripes we are healed.
Isaiah 53:3-5

This is what true leadership is all about. It involves bearing the pains and the sorrows of the people, making you as a leader who would spend all night and day to inquire of the Lord what wisdom is needed to turn their situations from deadness to life. We are going to go into the various sub-doctrines that make up the doctrine of true leadership, explaining them in detail so that we can be equipped to become true leaders who are out to execute the will of God on earth. These sub-doctrines, as dictated to me by inspiration, are captured in the successive chapters of this book.

CHAPTER THREE

LEADERSHIP AUTHORITY

Leadership is all about authority. This is the reliance on the power of God that comes into our lives (1 Corinthians 1:24). What gives us authority is knowing who we are. Knowing who you are or ought to be requires that you are in tune with your creator, and that you know exactly your purpose on earth.

This is where the problem is with many of us. We don't know why we are where we are, or why we do the things we do. Life is a continuum, which means one action will normally lead to another. We have chemical chain reactions in chemistry, and nuclear activities are based on this phenomenon of reactivity.

Since authority comes with knowledge, a leader must seek to equip the people he/she leads with knowledge at every point in time (Jeremiah 3:15). To do this, the leader must first be equipped. The Bible says the Government will be upon His shoulder. For this to happen, that leader must be like God Himself in perfection (Matthew 5:48), which is the only reason why it is only God that can give the kind of sacrifice that is enough to save a crooked world like ours.

Authority is the ability to provide effective counsel. The doctrine of authority therefore can be summarised in the following reasoning.

KNOWLEDGE

A leader must be knowledgeable enough to lead others. The Bible says the blind cannot lead the blind (Luke 6:39). Adam failed because he was not knowledgeable enough to have communicated spiritual details to Eve, who was ready to help him. Eve may have been left to herself alone, while Adam walked about the garden, tendering it alone, without involving Eve. Then Eve's eyes caught the fruit of the tree again. The fruit was pleasant and the devil had sown in her heart that the fruit will be delicious, and she ate it and gave to her husband. The husband couldn't stop at that point; he ate it with her. This is the failure in leadership we are talking about.

Esther 1:22 says that every man should be in control of his household. When the chips were down, Adam couldn't assume his position as the head, but he blamed his foolishness and lack of authority on his wife. To me, as I said earlier, this is where man lost his gift of leadership.

The government must be upon the shoulder of every leader, implying that he/she must consider the joy of the people he/she is leading first. It is a difficult process to transform people, because they won't want to move to the new doctrine you will be teaching them.

Before you can take authority, you must have understanding about what you do. For instance, even if I can give you a job, before you can have an understanding that a job is coming your way, you must know what I am about to do. The choir, for instance, can only become perfect when they are able to take authority and command, and must be confident of the parts they must all play to ensure we hear music instead of mere sound or noise. This is why they need to pass through some form of training and gain some knowledge. They need to make sacrifices and throw away all they've known before they can be able to learn.

A leader must be knowledgeable enough to lead others. The husband has knowledge of ruling his house, and the same thing applies to the wife who is managing the home, otherwise the home will be in pieces. If you want people to admire, respond and respect you in whatever you are doing, they must be knowledgeable and ready to adopt a superior knowledge to that which they had learned before. You need knowledge to be able to lead people well. The Bible says, the blind cannot lead the blind. You must have the requisite knowledge to lead effectively.

In whatever you want to do, try and seek more knowledge

so you that you will know how to do it better. You are seeking knowledge because you want to do things better, more efficiently, and save time. You can save a lot of money, time and energy when you are able to acquire the right knowledge.

The church is an easy place to acquire knowledge, where you don't need any payment. If you are to go for leadership training in a very big organisation, you could be paying a thousand dollars or more. This is one of the reasons we have to study the Bible and hear from God's servants, as they open our understanding of the secret leadership qualities the Bible has to offer.

COUNSEL

Counselling is an offshoot of knowledge. Leaders who counsel with results are those who are equipped with both spiritual and physical knowledge. St Paul's counselling is a demonstration of his experience and wisdom.

The proverbs in the Bible are borne out of knowledge. The Bible says in Proverbs 15:22 that counsel establishes leadership purpose of direction and vision: 'without counsel purposes are disappointed: but in the multitude of counsellors they are established.' While growing up, I used to hear the elders say that a housefly that has no adviser will follow the corpse to the grave.

A leader is expected to be able to counsel people and get

feedback from them. If you are not a leader there is no way you can advise others or take advice from them. You are a leader when you are not easily led astray. You should know what advice to take and what to discard. This is where you need the help of the spirit of God.

Your ability to counsel, listen and advise others will make you discover that some day you will be somebody of influence in life. We suffer because many of us have lost these leadership qualities, and this came from Adam, when he could not accept the blame for being responsible for his fall. Rather he told God 'the woman you gave me.' Many of us, when we see things going wrong or an accident waiting to happen, start asking questions about who is responsible, instead of thinking of how to put things right. Many of us have failed as leaders due to the fact that we blame our failures on people, especially those we lead.

We should analyse what went wrong after intervention before a leader can counsel effectively. Until you learn how to advise people successfully you cannot become a leader. In anything you are going to do, be it business, seeking for contracts, marriage, etc, if you cannot lead yourself you can't lead people. A counsellor must have enough experience, and to be experienced, you must have some fundamental knowledge. This is why the Holy Spirit is filled with counsel, because He has been around from the beginning of creation

(Genesis 1:2), giving Him so much experience of people and how they live. So He has enough advice to give to you.

From this fact about the Holy Spirit, we see that without knowledge, there is no leadership counsel in place. For instance, everybody knows that any girl who is ripe for marriage must know how to cook, dress the home, love her husband, etc – that is fundamental, but when the girl doesn't know all these things, she needs counselling from someone who does. A person must know how to counsel his friends, as they depend on the kind of advice you are giving them to make them shine and feel happy. A disciple cannot guide other disciples, only a leader can do so. The only way you can guide others is when you have leadership qualities in you and people will come after you – this is leadership counsel in action.

My marriage to my wife was as a result of her advice to me, and she is one of those whose advice made me who I am today. When I told her I wanted to marry her, I was ready to show an example, letting her know I can be the man she deserves.

A leader is someone who can provide the necessary needs of the people he/she leads through counselling. You must have the spirit of counsel to lead people well. You should not see everybody you lead after a period of time as being wrong - if you do, your leadership is wrong. Everybody cannot be wrong. If we were we would all be heading for destruction and the leader is already doomed.

I can only take you to where I am going. If someone is in a pit and you want them out, if he or she is not ready yet then they may make sure you fall into the pit with them. If someone is up and dragging you up, then you will be up before you know it. When you see somebody who is unable to lead people well, check the person – he is already going astray.

DISCIPLINE

Discipline sets in automatically once there is leadership authority. I have seen leaders who are not disciplined. Discipline also relies on the level of knowledge residing in a leader. Discipline comes with maturity, as one treads the path of the known to the unknown, where the skill of leadership is most needed. God promised to lead us in Isaiah 42:16:

And I will bring the blind by a way that they knew not; I will lead them in paths that they have not known: I will make darkness light before them, and crooked things straight. These things will I do unto them, and not forsake them.

To lead a blind man requires discipline. Your ability to lead the kind of people God referred to above comes automatically, when you have knowledge of who they are and the knowledge they need to experience the light you are about to lead them into. Otherwise they will rebel and hate you as you try to make them change from their comfort level to a higher level of appreciation, where they will become stars that would shine in darkness.

There are people who have authority but are not disciplined - they come late to the office or church and are not accountable for what they are doing. They are not ready and do not need questioning. I once heard of some students who were afraid that their results would be sent directly to their parents and guardians, so they started giving fake addresses which did not lead anywhere. When the school sent their results, they would be returned undelivered. Instead of trying to increase their performance they decided to deceive the authority, for fear of their parents seeing their results. Such acts will make them remain where they were, because of indiscipline.

Discipline will make you adjust, reduce your expenses to suit your income, and you will manage and take charge of your life by thinking ahead. If you are disciplined, you will learn to ensure that you don't finish everything you earn at once. It will make you respect yourself wherever you are and see yourself as an image of God. Discipline will make you know you need to solve the problem now, without waiting for tomorrow.

Whenever the right, disciplined people head a government institution or take the helm of affairs, wherever they may be, things seem to work like magic. When Buhari and Idiagbon came into power in Nigeria, they came with War Against Indiscipline (WAI) and everybody was shouting.

This discipline could be seen when people were made not to throw dirt anywhere or park their cars wrongly along the highway. In the office, people are often told not to eat food in the office because of rodents, but they won't listen and rats flood everywhere. People want to be monitored and thoroughly supervised before they can do the right thing. Even at that, they fear punishment more than mere advice. Punishment terms bring discipline into action in those you lead. On the highway, you will notice that drivers quickly reduce their speed when they see the Road Safety Corps on duty, yet they have driven past dozens of road signs giving the speed limit. Drivers are arrested for traffic offences as a result of indiscipline.

As a student, discipline begins at home. If you are disciplined your teachers don't need to use the rod on you. Some children run inside to pretend to be reading their books when they hear the horn of their father's car. That is indiscipline, and if they continue like that they will fail their exams and will definitely become failures as leaders. Indiscipline in leadership is the root of leadership failures.

PATIENCE

Patience is another attribute of authority. Those who are hasty can hardly lead people into proven success. Jesus taught us that in patience we possess our souls (Luke 21:19).

I once worshipped in a local church with less than ten members. The pastor of that small church changed my life for good. He said: 'No land is dry, only pray not to encounter dry people. Dry people have nothing to offer, any time you are with them, all you hear is stories of disappointments and why it is difficult for you to attain your height in life - they have all the stories of failed people at their finger tips. Run from them and hope in Jesus, He endured the cross to obtain the crown of everlasting kingship. Endure yours today - smile is ahead.' Since then, my life has never remained the same.

Patience is another attribute of leadership. You need not be in a hurry in what you do as a leader. Hurry makes it difficult for us to receive the knowledge and information we need in order to grow. We all went to school, but how many can testify that we actually went through the school and learned all we were supposed to learn in line with the academic syllabus? Can we also say that our parents took good care of us and fed us with the knowledge we need to survive? This is a fact of life.

Patience is the reason you would want to sit down on the floor for somebody to teach you. It is the reason why you will wait and pray until God answers, but when you are impatient you start moving from one church to the other and not believing the teaching you are hearing. We are here, in this world, to grow teachers. As leaders, you must strive on to see the end before you move on. There is nothing you cannot do with patience.

Just watch and pray, be careful, gentle, work and you will discover that you are getting there. When you run fast, after some time you begin to pant, because you've lost your breath. You also begin to sweat profusely, become uncomfortable and look for how to cool yourself down. This was the story of the race between the tortoise and the hare which many of us were told while growing up.

RELIABILITY

Reliability is another attribute of leaders who have the authority to take those they lead into their promised inheritance. Joshua was reliable, and the people trusted him because he had the right wisdom upon him (Deuteronomy 34:9). You cannot be a reliable leader when you don't have knowledge, and you cannot have authority until you have knowledge. Reliability is the product of understanding. The breath of God is what brings understanding, so we can confidently say that when a leader is out of tune with God, he loses stability and becomes unreliable. Leadership reliability has a lot to do with spiritual balance.

If you are not reliable and people are relying on you, there is no way you can succeed in life trying to carry your admirers along. If you are reliable people can trust you, if not people will not believe, trust or come closer to you or work with you.

Bosses writes their remarks about their staff on a yearly basis, and that results in the yearly ranking. In the office, sometimes I have been referred to as reliable, and in some cases the report says they can see a lot of potential in me, but it seems not to be coming out. On other occasions they have written that they could see the attribute of high integrity in me. All these kinds of appraisals help a growing leader to become firmer in his/her pursuit of stability and reliability. People want those who can deliver, and deliverability is linked to reliability. God will ask at the last day and we will all account for everything we've been doing. If you are an unreliable member of staff, you are on your way out. People are looking for people who are reliable, people who can give you their word, they'll tell you what they will do and then do it accordingly, to their promise of deliverables. When you are reliable, people will wait for you. If I can trust you, I will lay my life for you. Christ laid down his life for you; can God say you are reliable? That you are somebody He can give information and that you will use it to beautify his world? If you are not reliable, God cannot work with you.

CONFIDENCE

Confidence is the next attribute of authoritative leaders. You must have confidence in yourself before people can have confidence in you. In Proverbs 14:26, the Bible says that confidence can only come when we fear God. And also in Proverbs 9:10, we are taught that the fear of God is the beginning of wisdom. And wisdom, we also know from the Proverbs 9:1, is founded on seven pillars. These pillars are the seven spirits of God (Isaiah 11:2).

A leader must be very confident of his leadership goals. If you don't believe in yourself, you cannot make others believe in you. God has called many of us into his vineyard, but many don't trust in the power of God, so we cannot really deliver because we don't believe God can take us there. We now go from one native doctor to the other looking for solution, as many pastors do to increase membership in their church. If the business is God's, why not wait on Him? When God called you into his vineyard, he will cause a flood around you, to destabilise those old filthy relationships that you previously had, and you must have the heart to accept it.

The flood therefore has to take place for there to be perfection, and for the church to have a form. If the church has no form, God must cause something to happen so that there will be form and shape, and we can work in an environment where we have form and order.

When you fear God you will be confident of His commands and know in your heart that the commands in the Bible are truly from God. And when you are confident that when you really obey God, you will get to where you are going. You will overcome every obstacle on your way to leadership heights of achievement. When you don't fear Him, you will not believe and trust Him. God is our confidant. A leader who leads without the backing of God is set to fail.

TEMPERAMENT

Temperament control is an act of maturity in the faith we profess. Ability to control our temperament shows that we have authority. The empty can, they say, makes the loudest noise. While growing up in the village, the elders will always say that a short man or woman will try to disagree with everything said so that they are noticed. In Proverbs 14:17, we are taught that a quick-tempered man acts foolishly. Anyone who acts foolishly cannot claim to have authority. We are told to go back to God whenever we are faced with obstacles that seem not to get out of our way. This is because God is the source of every leader's authority. When leaders lack this connection into the realm of the spirit it becomes difficult for them to sail through the crocodile-infested waters of temptation.

Controlling your anger comes with maturity, meaning that your ability to control your anger comes with how mature you are, and you can't be mature when you don't have knowledge. That is why teaching about a life subject is good, either in the church or some other moral institution. Be attentive and after the teaching, find a way of getting the recorded message, if it exists, and listening to it again. When you listen over and over again, you become matured in the wisdom contained in the message. This will help you to control your anger when you encounter similar situations, and you are set to succeed in life, because the people you are going to work with don't want to work with a leader who is arrogant.

If you are the angry type, people will run away from you. The Bible says it is better to stay in a desert than to stay with a nagging woman (Proverbs 21:19). If you are a nagging woman your husband will leave home as he tries to secure peace. If you are quick-tempered, all your actions will become foolish (Proverbs 14:17) and as long as you act foolishly, you will not receive positive results.

Imagine you in an office and your boss tell you to tidy up the office, and while you are trying to do this you receive a phone call which makes you angry. Will you arrange the office properly? No! When you get angry, go inside, take a deep breath and come out and start your work again. If you can control your anger, you can act wisely.

You should be asking yourself a question: why do you go for a job and find it is offered to somebody else? Maybe during the interview they were looking for the ability to work in a team.

When you are in the house of God it is time to repent so that you can grow into maturity. You are supposed to grow so you can start teaching other people the authority in the name of Jesus. At any time it will be useful if you ask yourself a question, to be sure of why you come to the church every Sunday. Did you come because other people are coming? It is only a fool who does not have a reason for what he or she does. Those who marry because everybody else is marrying are not wise.

I often tell congregations that it is not about how many children you have, it is why you had them. Sarah had just one child, Isaac, and that Isaac is the father of Christianity today. It is not about the many contracts a contractor has, it is about the quality of the job they will deliver. If you are not a man who values quality, your wife will not bother about you that much, because she knows that anything goes as far as you are concerned. Something that will pay you extra money is hinged on quality and not quantity.

As leaders, we must ask ourselves simple questions about what we are doing. A wife, for instance, who is cooking in the kitchen, should have it at the back of her mind that her husband should love the food she is busy preparing. I don't blame people for blame's sake when they tend to err while working with me. I always feel maybe I haven't done enough and lived by example, yet. When you begin to do that, you see that people get closer to you. All the things you used to complain about will stop and you can now work with them in respect. If you always shout at your workmen, check yourself - maybe you have not lived by example. Show some commitment, draw out your plan and let them have their input into it – only then will it become a working plan. We need to first of all train ourselves up, because when you are unable to do this any hand you are stretching to the other person may be filthy and smelly. You need to learn at all times.

Many people have left our church because they don't want me to preach a message that talks to them about their ill characters, and are seen outside getting worse than they were. When they came to join our church, after a few months, they were getting better in life and growing in wisdom, but later they left, angry that I was revealing their secrets during my preaching that they were visiting divination prophets who only deceive them.

INTEGRITY

God wants to father a generation of humans who will be as perfect as He is (Matthew 5:48). This is the whole essence of why God is interested in turning our hearts back to Him, the way it was before the fall of man.

I want to take your mind back to the Ten Commandments. This is a set of rules which was meant to address the negativity in the lives of the Israelites, after being slaves in the land of Egypt for 430 years. As slaves, there was no way they could be as God intended since they are supposed to be heirs of His kingdom. So God had to turn their hearts first to Him, and integrity is all God was after.

The problem the children of Israel had was that they saw the Ten Commandments as self sustaining, without them submitting their hearts to God. We all have characters we need to change; these characters also form part of the commandments, in our case, which we need to adhere to. Some of us have more than Ten Commandments to observe, maybe seventy times seven, as the case may be. Integrity, if seen as honesty, means we will love our neighbours as we love ourselves, and finally extend this love to God who created all of us. This is the issue with many of us, and we must repent from all our atrocities before God can be proud of us. This is the hallmark of integrity. This is why God always talked of justice, which the Jewish leaders were guilty of, which according to Christ is the weightier part of the law (Matthew 23:23). God considers integrity the number one principle every leader must keep to, and by extension, it also applies to those called by His name. We must be honest, straight forward, dedicated, and truthful, as leaders who serves to achieve positive results.

CHAPTER FOUR

LEADERSHIP ACCOUNTABILITY

Accountability goes with the call of duty. We have both spiritual and physical duty calls and both complement one another. Without a purposeful spiritual duty call, our physical exploits will always experience stagnation. I am going to talk about the most important duty call for man recorded in the Bible, and all other duty calls are offshoot of this. They can be found in the books of Joshua 1:6 and Luke 4:18-19:

Be strong and of a good courage: for unto this people shalt thou divide for an inheritance the land, which I swear unto their fathers to give them.

The Spirit of the Lord is upon me, because he hath anointed me to preach the gospel to the poor; he hath sent me to heal the brokenhearted, to preach deliverance to the captives, and recovering of sight to the blind, to set at liberty them that are bruised.

Let us take a look at the verses above. Two leaders have been called to duty and their duties point to one fact - restoration. We have job titles in our workplaces which outline our own contribution to the overall success of the company as seen in the company's statement of business policies. What job title did God gave to us? Jesus taught us in Matthew 28:19-20 that we are disciples of a higher calling, who have the spirit of Christ in us. And if the spirit of Christ lives in us we will surely know our duty posts. Accountability is tied to our job titles. The title 'wife' qualifies the woman as the rightful and legitimate child bearer of her husband. Any child born by the man outside her matrimonial home is seen as illegitimate. So the woman's accountability to bear children in the home is related to her title as the wife.

Let's see this verse in the Bible, Matthew 10:30: 'But the very hairs of your head are all numbered'. This tells us of the task involved for us to be able to give full account of all that we do. Counting the hairs in one's head is a strenuous job. The fact that leadership accountability is strenuous is all the more reason why staff find it difficult to give realistic progress reports. Many would taint the report to prove to their leaders that they are achieving more than planned. Review meetings have been boycotted by some with the excuse that they are ill. I have also heard of financial records been mutilated to agree with what management have agreed prior to commencement of the job. Fraud is committed by people in an attempt to give account of how they have spent the resources they planned to have spent on specific job assignments. Many have also tried to bribe audit teams to save their faces. Document centres have been set ablaze in some instances, to ensure that there was no evidence to indict them of leadership malpractices. This is how accountability bites.

Let us see how Jesus gave account of what He was doing to those sent to Him by John, in Matthew 11:4-5: 'Jesus answered and said unto them, Go and shew John again those things which ye do hear and see: The blind receive their sight, and the lame walk, the lepers are cleansed, and the deaf hear, the dead are raised up, and the poor have the gospel preached to them.' Accountability means proven evidence. Jesus had all the evidence around Him to show the 'auditors', so to speak, who had come with the message from John: 'Now when John had heard in the prison the works of Christ, he sent two of his disciples, and said unto him, art thou he that should come, or do we look for another?' (Matthew 11:2-3). Accountability is more of a 'show me' affair.

I also discovered something during the early days of my ministry; that whenever I was not around my members seemed to leave things unkempt. Even in my house there is always something that will go wrong when I am not there. I have also seen that many purportedly claiming to be believers are interested in long hours of prayers without winning souls, even when the Bible says that the soul winner is wise.

One obligation I know the church leaders have is to pray

for harvesters in the Lord's vineyard. Yet how many of us do this? I really believe that we should pray for our personal needs, but we need more than that. Our prayers should be against temptation, while we need to think more about recruiting disciples. Evangelism is all we need to grow. I have seen ministries who pray little but go out more in winning souls, and they are more successful than those who sit all day long hiding in their weakness for evangelism, all in the name of praying.

All these failures on our path to evangelise boil down to the lack of the understanding of our accountability before God. What then is accountability? The term is taken from two English words; account and ability. It is the ability of leaders to give detailed account or stewardship of their roles and responsibilities, in respect to their calling. It is the heart of the ability of leaders to take responsibility for their actions. It is an ethical term, and therefore defines leadership ethics.

We have, in Christianity, the doctrine of the Christian virtues of faith, hope and love. This is the basic principle of Christian leadership accountability. Many leaders don't want to be accountable to anybody. This is how you differentiate a leader from a boss; a leader is accountable to God and those he/she leads. Why should every leader be accountable to God? Because the people they lead were created in the image and likeness of God. They are God's handiwork. So anyone who is saddled with the responsibility of leading God's children should do so with a heart of submission unto God.

Leadership conscience is a term I want us to digest as we talk about accountability. Accountability can either be obligatory or non-obligatory. Here also we have both spiritual and physical obligation. Accountability is wholly obligatory when it has to do with God. We all must give account someday (Hebrew 11:6). In our daily lives, we are also accountable to our loved ones, in our workplaces – our bosses. But it may be obligatory or non-obligatory. It is obligatory that my wife knows me in and out, including my estates, but if my wife is an enemy in disguise, then that obligation is questionable. This then also boils down to trust.

To this end, we will be seeing leadership accountability in the following light:

- Visibility is the first attribute of every leader. A leader who hides from the people he/she leads is not a leader but a devourer. It is only the devouring animal, like the lion that will be hiding from its prey until it can launch an attack to end the life of the prey - John 14:8-9.

- A leader must possess the power of attraction, what people will call charisma. –Matthew 4:18-20.

- A leader must know that he/she has tenure of office and after that he/she will hand over to another, who must run with the vision. Elijah failed here. He knew already that

Elisha was to be his successor but he never gave the mantle until Elisha followed, risking his own life. Leaders shouldn't behave like this; they must be willing to share information and knowledge all the time, to ensure there is continuity. This is Jesus' example - John 14:12-14.

- A leader must be result driven. He/she must ensure that every second of the clock is invested in actualising the objective of the vision and not on self-aggrandizement. - Matthew 5:17.

- A leader must accept criticisms and critiques from people, even those he leads. They should be able to know those who pay eye service to them, because with these sets of people, he/she is certainly going to fail. Jesus was questioned several times by his disciples and He pointed them to the facts of His leadership.

- A leader should have answer to every question that is put towards him/her. What does this mean? It does not mean he/she is a 'know-all', but they should know what is going on in wherever they find themselves.

- Must be precise in action – Luke 8:45-46.

- Should know those who work with them – Luke 8:20-21, Matthew 27:46.

Leadership accountability spans the spheres of moral accountability, administrative accountability, pastoral accountability, and followership accountability. Let us discuss them in turn:

1. Moral accountability

Moral accountability is tied to integrity. Every leader must operate within some ethical framework, to guide him and provide a form of checks and balance in all his actions. He must operate at all times as a sane person. The Bible taught us that a leader must be temperate in all things. This is where his honour as a leader will come from. It is my candid advice that every leader should carry out moral accountability assessment on their actions. The Bible also said of Jesus in Isaiah 42:2,3: 'He will not cry out, nor raise His voice, nor cause His voice to be heard in the street. A bruised reed he will not break...' This is moral accountability.

2. Administrative accountability

Administration has to do with how a leader is able to put his vision across to those he leads, and the daily management of the vision he is driving to know that he is still within course. It has to do with the sourcing of the right resources, both human and material. This will be possible through the availability of finance. The parable of the talents explained what financial accountability is all about (Matthew 25:14-30).

Another area of administrative accountability is legal accountability. A leader must ensure that he operates within the laws that govern the state where he operates. Jesus demonstrated this in His payment of tax (Matthew 17:26-27). This is why churches register their trustees, and depending on the laws governing the religious association in a state, the church may or may not have public crusades. A leader is an administrator and he must be responsible enough to make acceptable financial and legal judgements.

3. Pastoral accountability

The act of leadership is likened to pastoring. A pastor oversees the church, meeting its physical and spiritual needs. A leader who sees himself performing the role of a pastor would know how to seek God when things are not right with his leadership responsibilities.

Many leaders fail to perform simply because they don't see themselves as spiritual leaders. Let us consider the governor of a state for instance, since he has to stand before God's children to tell them what he has planned to do which would go a long way in affecting the people's lives, emotionally and spiritually. Such a person must have a spiritual relationship with God. It is my opinion that every leader must undergo pastoral training before holding public offices. This will enable them to have the fear of God, watch their lies, and be more accountable to the course of the vision they would drive, so that the people they are going to lead rejoice. If we imbibe this advice, it won't be long before we start having the righteous in the corridors of power and that will mean that such a state or nation will have the fear of God since the leader already does, and God's blessings will fall on everyone like the dew from heaven.

4. Followership accountability

A leader who sees his responsibility to lead with a sense of followership will always be humble. A humble leader is always ready to serve others and this is what will make people follow him wherever he goes, driving his vision.

The Bible says that Moses was the most humble in his days - Numbers 12:3: 'Now the man Moses was very humble, more than all men who were on the face of the earth'. This humility is seen in his help to the daughters of the Midian Priest, without demanding a reward or assistance, even when he had no place to lay his head because he was a fugitive fleeing from the face of Pharaoh: 'Then the shepherds came and drove them away; but Moses stood up and helped them, and watered their flock' (Exodus 2:17). This is the heart of a leader. Every leader should be able to do an assessment of how they render assistance to those who are helpless. This will enable them to know the extent of their ability to lead.

Followership characteristics include volunteering to handle tasks, putting on a positive attitude all the time in order not to be in the bad books of the master, dedication to duty, willingness to assist others etc. All these would be seen in the lives of the disciples of Jesus as they preached the gospel of Christ after His resurrection.

CHAPTER FIVE

LEADERSHIP ASSOCIABILITY

The Bible says in Isaiah 9:6 that Jesus is a child and a son to everyone. This is what spells out what we will be talking about.

Associability is simply the ability to associate. We associate when we lead, because we meet people daily from different culture and walks of life. When Jesus called His disciples to Himself, he barely knew them, but the principle of associability was the reason He was able to walk and work with them for three years. After His ascension, because of this same quality, He, through the Holy Spirit, manifested His presence in them daily, confirming what He said in John 14:19, that they would see him but the world cannot see Him.

Noah Webster's American Dictionary of the English Language, published in 1828, defines associability as 'The quality of being capable of association; the quality of suffering some change by sympathy, or of being affected by the affections of another part of the body'. Associability transcends the different layers of societal personalities: the wealthy, the middle class and the poor. Christ's example teaches us this. Joseph of

Arimathea, who buried Jesus, was wealthy, and Nicodemus, the Jewish teacher, was a middle class citizen; both of them were well to do. Peter was a fisherman, surviving on what he caught, and Mary was an adulterous woman, caught in the very act. This is what the definition above is saying. One must have the quality of association and not discrimination. When we discriminate, we end up not being able to lead well.

All effective leaders know how to subject themselves into a state that will make them feel the pains that others are going through. Saint Paul said that he became all things to all men, in 1 Corinthians 9:19-23:

19 *For though I be free from all men, yet have I made myself servant unto all, that I might gain the more.*

20 *And unto the Jews I became as a Jew, that I might gain the Jews; to them that are under the law, as under the law, that I might gain them that are under the law;*

21 *To them that are without law, as without law, (being not without law to God, but under the law to Christ,) that I might gain them that are without law.*

22 *To the weak became I as weak, that I might gain the weak: I am made all things to all men, that I might by all means save some.*

23 *And this I do for the gospel's sake, that I might be partaker thereof with you.*

Here Paul made it clearer that in order to be like Jesus, who died for the gospel's sake, we must all learn to associate with others for the sake of preaching the gospel. Jesus' pattern of associability is born out of the fact that He sees them all as children of God, with no special treatment to any of these sets of people. The Bible taught us that the Lord God created them all. The Anglican hymn reads:

1. All things bright and beautiful,
    All creatures great and small,
    All things wise and wonderful,
    The Lord God made them all.

2. Each little flower that opens,
    Each little bird that sings,
    He made their glowing colours,
    He made their tiny wings.

3. The rich man in his castle,
    The poor man at his gate,
    God made them high and lowly,
    And ordered their estate.

'The Lord God made them all.' This is what should be ringing in the mind of every leader who is ready to succeed.

Neglecting any of the social classes in the group that he leads, and failing to know that these groups have different needs, could mean chaos in our attempts at leadership.

In the church for instance, these sets of groups often flock together more often, and any attempt to make the lower class feel intimidated by the show of affluence, or the show of extreme intelligence by the elite, can brew hatred and seamlessness in the various groups and meetings in the church. This is where the heart of a leader comes in. With the guidance of the Holy Spirit, He ensures that no group feels unrecognised. An inferiority complex is an outcome of lack of associability.

The story of Esau and Jacob tells us of the cost of lack of associability. Esau, as the eldest, was supposed to have been the right leader in the house. Even while he was such a skilled hunter, his inability to associate effectively with his brother cost him his birthright. If not why would Jacob demand his birthright or anything before giving him food? To him, like many, birthright was just a number and he never saw the spiritual importance of it.

Many leaders seldom undermine their years of experience, or fail to pick up learning as the days goes by. Esau would have known on time that his brother was playing a fast game on him, else why would Jacob ever demand his birthright?

Once a leader lose track of these strata of human

existence, he/she is on his/her way down. To the needy and poor, Jesus Christ lived a life, and instituted, a ministry of compassion:

1. He joined with them occasionally, mingling with them (Luke 5:1-11)

2. He ate with them, in their midst (Luke 5:27-32),

3. He comforted them and shared in their burden (Luke 12:22-34),

4. He, even, fed them as God did to the Israelites when He provided manna for them (Luke 9:10-17),

5. Many were healed by Him (Luke 5:12-16), and

6. He taught them, ministering to their needs; spiritually and physically (Luke 7:18-23).

This is associability at work. To the elite, he counselled them, and employed them; Luke was a medical doctor, Paul a lawyer, Zacchaeus a tax man, Matthew a tax collector, etc. Even the soldiers had His attention - the centurion servant was healed, and the rich, Joseph of Arimathea who buried Him, and the religious, Nicodemus, had a tête-à-tête with Him also, because He became their solution at the point of their imminent needs.

Jesus' central message was associability. One instance of this is seen in Matthew 5:21-24:

You have heard that it was said to those of old, 'You shall not murder, and whoever murders will be in danger of the judgment'. But I say to you that whoever is angry with his brother without a cause shall be in danger of the judgment. And whoever says to his brother, 'Raca!' shall be in danger of the council. But whoever says, 'You fool!' shall be in danger of hell fire. Therefore if you bring your gift to the altar, and there remember that your brother has something against you, leave your gift there before the altar, and go your way. First be reconciled to your brother, and then come and offer your gift.

All these point to the fact that Jesus saw the need for reconciliation and knew how this would enhance the vision of restoration He came to die for.

There is a principle that helps in associability and that is what I call Leadership step-out. This is when a leader sees the need to connect his little world with the larger society, just as a pastor would see his pastorage as a home for counselling, so that all and sundry will come to know the vision he is driving. He also ensures that those working with him are carried along. Jesus displayed this associability attribute when His ministry became known all over the land of Israel and beyond. Everyone also knew who His disciples were, without which the Bible wouldn't have recorded their names. A leader who steps out of His microcosm is one whose leadership legacy will stand the test of time. No matter what good work you are doing as a leader, it is time to announce it, so that the public know what you and your organisation stand for.

In the book of Judges 7, we would see that for someone like Gideon to raise 32,000 soldiers shows that those who went out with him to fight knew exactly what their goal was. This is leadership step-out in action.

Now let's look at some Bible verses below, so as to get a deeper understanding of what we are talking about.

Ingredients needed by the leader for Associability to work:

• **Love:** To love is to care. There is no one who senses this act in a leader that would not be ready to lend a helping hand to his vision. The Bible says that we love God because he loved us first: 'We love because he first loved' -1 John 4:19. And the outcome as represented by this verse is, 'we love.' A leader with the heart that loves will always experience love blossoming among those he leads.

• **Clarity of purpose:** Many people find it difficult to associate with a leader because they find it difficult to understand the purpose of the vision he is driving. Jesus explained in clear terms the reason why He came to earth, in John 18:37: 'Pilate therefore said to Him, 'Are You a king then?' Jesus answered, 'You say rightly that I am a king. For this cause I was born, and for this cause I have come into the world, that I should bear witness to the truth. Everyone who is of the truth hears My voice'.'

• **Selfless service:** When those you lead see you as a leader who serves selflessly, they would be ready to support you to ensure that you succeed. Selfless service attracts the poor and rich alike. You would see them running down to have a bond of relationship with you. People saw how King Solomon was dedicative to the building of the temple of God, and they travelled across lands and seas to associate with him.

• **Humility:** A humble leader is like sugar that attracts ants. Every ant comes there to have a grain of the sugar and goes away. This is what humility looks like. Jesus said that He was meek and lowly (Matthew 11:29), meaning that He was extremely humble – becoming poor for the sake of restoring mankind back to God. He endured the shame to bring us salvation. This is the beauty of humility. We would see how He attracted everyone to Himself. Everyone would want a humble person for a leader. Humility cannot be practised but lives within, spanning years of discipline and upbringing.

• **Chastity:** A leader should be trusted by the opposite sex not to be one who would lure them to bed. Even in the way they look in their eyes should not be seen as a passion display. Jesus says: 'But I say to you that whoever looks at a woman to lust for her has already committed adultery with her in his heart.' – Matthew 5:28. Leaders should avoid lustful desires. Chastity in a leader will breed the association of everybody – male and female supporting the leader to succeed.

• **Charisma:** A leader with an alluring personality will always win the hearts of people who admire his leadership prowess. This is why a leader must look handsome and astute. His dressing, though it may not be expensive, should be neat and well ironed. Joseph was given a coat of many colours and he indeed became a leader. The clothes you wear have a way of announcing your leadership gift to the world.

• **Boldness:** A bold leader is ready to confront evil practices or wrongdoings in public. Jesus spoke boldly: Jesus answered him, 'I spoke openly to the world. I always taught in synagogues and in the temple, where the Jews always meet, and in secret I have said nothing. Why do you ask Me? Ask those who have heard Me what I said to them. Indeed they know what I said.'- John 18:20-21. The act of boldness is the reason why a leader will stand up to make know his intentions and decisions. A non-decisive leader is not a bold leader, and such leaders often make little impact in the lives of those they lead.

• **Cleanliness:** A tidy environment attracts people. This is the secret of customer attraction. No one wants to live in an obnoxious environment. A leader should be aware of the fact. Clean surroundings, offices, seats, office electronics etc will bring people around you and your investments.

• **Beauty:** Apart from cleanliness, people often want to

associate themselves with beauty. The reason people travel for sightseeing is mostly because of the stories they have heard of how the areas people visited were beautiful. A beautiful home will always attract sightseers. As a leader, make sure you inject beauty into everything you do, from your signposts and posters, the books you write, the choice of cars you drive, etc. A little spark of beauty will bring people around you who would want to associate with you. Remember you are fearfully and wonderfully made.

• **Charity:** The Bible says that a man's gift makes a way for him, Proverbs 18:16: A man's gift makes room for him, And brings him before great men. The last line says that charity brings us before great people. This is associability at work. A leader who wants increase must be ready to give something for the sake of charity, and the society will seek after him. I would advice that any leader who wants greatness should first start by giving out donations for education, free journals, free health care etc.

• **Informed:** An informed leader is a point of attraction, as people cluster around him to be informed of events in the community. This is where his gift of teaching will eventually pay off. It will bring the high and low around him, provided he has a full grasp of the subject he talks about. As Jesus taught daily, his ministry grew as people flooded in from the surrounding gentile nations to hear him. We are told how he was always in the temple teaching.

• **Approachable:** People want a leader who they can easily approach. This means that to a large extent, a leader must operate an open-door policy, although this privilege is often misused. The disciples of Jesus had to institute a form of orderliness in those who wanted to see Jesus which could be seen in the act of the woman with the issue of blood. This did not deter people as someone like Zacchaeus in the Bible was attended to by Jesus, even when he had to climb a tree because of his height. If people see you as someone they can approach, they will flock around you.

• **Prosperity:** The Bible says that a poor man has no friends, Proverbs 19:4,7: 'Wealth makes many friends, But the poor is separated from his friend, All the brothers of the poor hate him; How much more do his friends go far from him!' Prosperity works likes a charm on everybody around you – even those who are far away. It has the power of magnetic attraction. A leader must desire to be prosperous if he/she wants recognition and association.

• **Leading by example:** People would want to associate with an exemplary leader. Whatever you want to be done should be exemplified by your actions and words. This is what builds the confidence of association in your followers or adherers.

CHAPTER SIX

LEADERSHIP ORDERLINESS

The reason for leadership at the helm of affairs is the doctrine of orderliness. Orderliness is the principle that has kept this earth rotating, without colliding with any other celestial body. Orderliness is the reason God gave the Israelites a pillar of fire by night and a pillar of cloud by day. Orderliness is the reason God said the Israelites must camp around Him (Numbers Chapter 2). God wants orderliness wherever His children may be.

We often read in the Bible how God's instructions were carried out according to how God ordered it by those that walked with Him. This shows that a leader must work according to a laid-down pattern. Non-orderly leaders will fail in every facet of leadership.

No leader who does not seek perfection can be orderly in their role, implying further that orderliness comes through perfection. This is why a leader who is difficult to train cannot be peaceful in life. The orderly leader hears a voice behind him and acts on it. In Isaiah 30:21, the prophet explains that it is not God's plan that we either go left or right, but to be focused in order to drive the vision ahead of us. In the leadership striving of Joshua we would see that God's instruction to him was: 'be thou courageous'.

The creation events in Chapter 1 of Genesis point to the advantage of being orderly. God started off with the creation of heaven and earth. He sent His spirit to envelop the deformed earth, and then filled the earth with illuminative wisdom and power, which we call light. He saw the goodness that this light brought; He then created a wall of separation between darkness – non-productive wisdom - and light, the productive wisdom. One after the other He created the elements of the world we live in today. Without the first creation being good, God never created another. He operated according to a set divine standard – no jumping the gun. Orderliness is a subject of reconciliation. What we see must reconcile with what we had imagined. This is God's principle. Let's see how this works out as we discuss further.

• **Wisdom** – Wisdom is the fruit of intelligence, and vice versa. One cannot exist without the other. This is what the orderly leader needs in order to plan what he is about to execute. He puts on an eagle-eye view so as to see ahead of time what he is about to achieve. Wisdom informs him how to store what he has seen in a form that can be easily interpreted by others. His striving is communication. Every decision must be based on an item in the plan so that he can achieve a bricklaying pattern which translates into walls of perfection that will stand free from all forms of imperfections. This is the reason why at the end of every bit of God's creation, he will inspect it to see that it is good and will become a foundation for another element.

The sea brought forth, the sky brought forth, and the earth brought forth. Every element of God's creation is productive. Even the mountains and rocky hills gave birth to the lowlands we see today through the process of erosion. So, we would see that though erosion is disadvantageous in one aspect - eroding farm lands, for instance, it is yielding new lands in another aspect. This is the wisdom of investment. An orderly leader knows exactly what fits into his plan. His mindset is filled with the wisdom of increase. Every part of the body must bear fruit. The Bible informs us that any branch of the vine that is not bearing fruit is pruned by God, to allow the conservation of nutrients to only the fruit-bearing branches (John 15:1-6). Wisdom will inform the orderly leader that it is time to conserve resources or expend resources. He watches needs and knows exactly what to do. His wisdom is filled with necessity. That is what drives an orderly leader.

- **Knowledge** – An orderly leader seeks knowledge from God through His words. He also searches available knowledge through consultation with experts in the subject area, filtering the information and knowing what to jettison in line with the goal he is achieving. There is a vision in every knowledge you gain. An orderly leader knows this and keeps it in his heart, knowing which knowledge to accept and which to reject in order to put his vision on the drive. All an orderly leader cares about is the effect of the knowledge he is pursuing and gaining on the vision he is driving.

God gave us what good knowledge can lead to when He said in 2 Kings 19:30: 'And the remnants who have escaped of the house of Judah shall again take root downward, and bear fruit upward'. Taking root downward is gaining the knowledge of the Lord, which will make them fear Him and render oblation unto Him from their hearts, and the act of bearing fruit upward is the outward manifestation of the effect of the knowledge gained to the success of the vision.

- **Understanding** – This is the rightful application of knowledge. An orderly leader will not learn a subject that will not be relevant to the goal he is pursuing. And when he thus learns them, he takes them to heart, to understand every facet of the knowledge gained, then he starts applying them, one after the other, learning from every previous trial. He engages those he leads to give feedbacks, and as he does this, he gets more understanding about the vision he is driving.

- **Vision** – An orderly leader is filled with vision. He sees ahead into years and years of fruitfulness. Jesus said that Abraham saw His days and rejoiced (John 8:56). This was the hope which gave Abraham that sense of balance as he walked through the length and breadth of the land God promised to give to him and his descendants. He saw the imperishable fruit of the tree that was at the centre of the Garden of Eden millions of years back, after Adam and Eve had been thrown out due to their act of disobedience. He may have been thinking: 'I wish I could lay my hands on that tree so that I could live forever.' And then he saw the one behind the tree. This is vision. An orderly leader will ensure that nothing takes him off course. He is guided by Isaiah 30:21: 'And thine ears shall hear a word behind thee, saying, This is the way, walk ye in it, when ye turn to the right hand, and when ye turn to the left.' He knows that he will hear a voice soon. So, he keeps waiting to hear, confirms that what he hears is in line with the dream he is pursuing, then acts. Here is the vision statement of my ministry: To be the general assembly and church of the firstborn which is written in heaven (Hebrew 12:22-24) – The Church that Overcometh (Revelations 3:5).

- **Mission** – I once watched a movie titled *Mission Impossible*. What came to my mind when I saw the title was why someone should embark on an impossible mission? The answer that rang in my head is that thorough research had not been done. Finally, in the movie, for the mission to be possible digital security codes had to be unravelled. This is what a mission statement does to a leader. They are the security lines of codes to make his mission possible.

Abraham heard the voice of the Lord, which ordered his footsteps, and that made him have a mission in life. Anyone with a mission knows where to tighten or loosen the nuts. A mission helps the leader to be orderly. Such missions should be precise and not vague. If you are going to visit the moon, your mission should state what you expect to achieve there. This is how an orderly leader thinks. The visit to the moon must have something to do with the vision.

Here is my ministry's mission statement: *To recruit, train and spiritually empower men, women, youths and children with the wisdom to execute God's Will on earth.* You will see that the mission is an instrument of the vision, through which the vision will be fulfilled. This mission is tied to what God expects from every child of His so that they can merit heaven.

Scripture tells us in Deuteronomy 34:9 that Joshua succeeded because he was filled with the spirit of wisdom. St Paul explains that this wisdom is Jesus (1 Corinthians 1:24). In Galatians 4:1-6 the Bible says that this wisdom must cry in your heart, but it has to be taught. And Jesus reiterated this fact, that it is only what we hear that can either clean us or dirty us (John 15:3).

The prophet Jeremiah hear God say that without His wisdom man would become ashamed and taken, emphasising eternal destruction. Jesus says that the will of God must be done so that mankind will experience the kingdom of God on Earth. So, building the blocks together, you will see where our mission statement came from. You can see orderliness in place from the mission statement. Our year-to-year plans are tied to the facts contained in our mission. Based on the mission statement, we have three major arms of the ministry: Giant Strides World Outreach Crusades (Recruit), School of Ministry (Train), Royal Diamonds International Church (Spiritual Empowerment). To make the mission statement live in my members' hearts, we gave it the acronym RTS. And we call this the three cardinal responsibilities of the Church, so they know what comes first – R, then T, and finally S. There is no way we can miss our train. RTS is all we would do to get to our vision. This is the heart of orderliness.

• **Discipline** – A leader may have a good mission statement, yet indiscipline on his part and those he leads can thwart his efforts to achieve seamless progress reports. What then is indiscipline? It is simply the act of disorderliness. It is the act of not following laid-down rules and regulation. For instance, a leader who does not know Christ should not preach salvation, else he will lead people astray. A man who does not have an idea of what marriage is all about should not be in marriage, else he will fail. Discipline is born out the need to judge accordingly, in line with available facts, turning them in one by one. Orderly leaders will act patiently. Jesus says that we can possess our soul – the power to reason productively if we are patient, Luke 21:19.

• **Compliance** – This creates checks and balances in his mind. He wants to comply with the dictates of the voice he hears behind – Isaiah 30:21. Setting a mission and vision statement is not enough. What makes you succeed as a leader is your compliance level to the values which you claim to uphold. What do you do when no one is watching? Would you want to still uphold the ethics of diligence or laxity to your calling? Jesus made mention of bearing fruits that would abide in John 15:16. This is compliance. How will the leader bear fruits that will endure every manner of challenges? It is only when he is connected to the vine of the power and wisdom of God – Jesus. We all know that Jesus was, indeed, an orderly leader. It therefore means that a leader who does not comply to laid-down rules and a regulation, including policies meant to ensure the vision succeeds, is not orderly.

• **Service oriented** – This is the hallmark of leadership. An orderly leader is service oriented. This is where his greatness is going to come from. All he thinks about is what he will do to make those he leads see the vision he is seeing. Then he puts himself into the line to test whatever ideas flow into his mind, ensuring that those he leads are not left in the dark as to what is to be done. As he sails through the leadership rough waters, he finds time to pause, to assess the progress made by others. When he is not getting the expected results, knowing that all those walking with him have a part to play in the vision he is driving, he steps into the situation, as Jesus calmed the sea for his disciples, and relieves everyone with him from the burden of failure, which tend to be insurmountable before them. This is the pulse of an orderly leader – all he sees and thinks about is how he can be of service to those he leads. Whoever he sees, what comes into his mind is: 'where can I help, or where do I come in?' He always want to do something that will add value.

- **Creativity** – Creativity can only thrive when there is orderliness. Creativity comes through thoughtful quietness. To be creative is to be orderly, because creativity is an act of problem solving. Leadership is all about problem solving. Someone has to take the lead to bring all the creative ideologies or school of thoughts into a pattern of ordered bricks of intelligence. A non-orderly leader can hardly engage in fruitful creativity. All his creative efforts are submerged in cowardice. He throws the stone before thinking what to aim at, and he will see that the Goliath he is suppose to bring down will keep advancing. A non-orderly leader creates holes in his creative ideas, and then experiences chaos in his leadership efforts. Creativity cannot exist without orderliness, just as orderliness cannot thrive without creativity. If you cage orderliness, you have caged creativity. Every orderly leader should give room for creativity in their administrative work, and their leadership ideals will span years of fruitfulness.

An orderly leader will rely on strategies. This is what makes the victor in a war. An array of soldiers, well positioned to defend and attack, shows real orderly skills. God tested Gideon's soldiers before he used them – this is orderliness. Our various academic lines of study show that one subject must come in first and be passed before one is given another and another until the expected knowledge is achieved or seen in us. We must be ready to undergo a dedicated training process to make us orderly in our thoughts and actions. An orderly thought leads to an orderly action and then to an orderly result. This why the Bible says that when the righteous rules, the people rejoice, because righteousness is the fruit of orderliness.

CHAPTER SEVEN

LEADERSHIP EQUITY

When the people brought in a woman caught in the very act, Jesus showed us what a leader should do before pronouncing judgement or taking a decision. He was calm even with the people shouting and demanding an instant answer. People should be given the opportunity to err. We are all human and prone to making mistakes.

King Solomon also demonstrated this in his judgement of the dead baby, and how he finally gave the live one to the rightful mother (1 Kings 3:16-28). The effective application of the principle of impartial judgement is what brings people together and grows an organisation. This will enable them to work and contribute their best in the team where they work. We must go back to the author of justice and fairness to understand what this subject is all about. Equity is a display of leadership. This is why Peter admired God's leadership principle of equity in Acts 10:34-35: 'Then Peter opened his mouth, and said, Of a truth I perceive that God is no respecter of persons: But in every nation he that feareth him, and worketh righteousness, is accepted with him'.

The conditions for enjoying justice and fair treatment within a leader's domain of influence is also stated in the above verse: respect and doing right, in line with stated rules and regulations, known as the commands of leadership. This is explained in Romans 13:3: 'For rulers are not a terror to good works, but to the evil. Wilt thou then not be afraid of the power? Do that which is good, and thou shalt have praise of the same'. How would a ruler know what to do so that his acts will not be seen as terrors? This is where he must have laid down laws checkmating his leadership prowess as he administers justice to those who errs. And he must be ready to pay the price of leading by example.

If a child errs, what do the parents do? Looking at the features of the male and female of every human being explains what equity is all about – one has what the other does not. God calls: 'Come let us reason together' (Isaiah 1:18). This is the heart of a leader. Everyone should be given the opportunity to speak out, to defend himself/herself against allegations, or acts of disobedience. No leader should pass judgement until the facts are clearly debated and it is certain, even in the eyes of the offender, that the law is right, and about to take its course.

The Bible also talks of someone being dead to sin (Romans 6:11), which means that we have obtained forgiveness through Christ. Yet Christ set some rules that we must obey to become dead to sin. This has to do with the laid-down rules and regulations of God's kingdom. The Laws of Moses guided the Jews for years, but the fault in its observance made God resolve to make a new law (Jeremiah 31:31-34). This is how a leader should act. Leadership is about review of how existing laws are being obeyed, and how to make them obey the laws without being afraid of them.

Leaders must submit themselves to public scrutiny for the purpose of accountability, as did Samuel, in 2 Samuel 12:21-23, so that he can prove that he was acting within the jurisdiction of his power, as permitted by law. God even said we should testify against Him, in Micah 6:3. No leader is above the law that governs where he rules. The causal factors that are responsible for a leader's incapacity to exercise true justice and fairness in their judgement are the lack of the fear of God and the respect for humanity.

Justice and fairness are the principles that bring the offender to book. To be able to understand justice and fairness let's take a look at how the originator of this principle, God Himself, explained this concept of leadership traits:

And surely your blood of your lives will I require; at the hand of every beast will I require it, and at the hand of man; at the hand of every man's brother will I require the life of man. Whoso sheddeth man's blood, by man shall his blood be shed: for in the image of God made he man. - Genesis 9:5-6.

This portion of the Bible explains what we will be discussing below. Justice is administered only when there is one who is found guilty. Not until he/she pleads guilty or is found guilty by a competent court of law is there justice. Competency in administering justice is borne out of the following:

Leading by example

A leader must live an exemplary life. He must be ready to face the music whenever he is culpable. In Nigeria, for instance, the immunity clause is making many leaders in power mismanage public funds. But it is not so with God. Whenever a leader errs in the Bible, God teaches them the bitter side of the law. He did it to Moses, King Saul, David, etc. God wants those who can lead by positive example. These are those he will refer us to for counselling. Jesus came to show us the heart of God: 'Think not that I am come to destroy the law, or the prophets: I am not come to destroy, but to fulfil.' - Matthew 5:17. Until He came to earth, mankind was finding it difficult to live according to the dictates of the laws of God.

Decisiveness

Being decisive does not mean being rude to those you lead. A decisive leader only does what is right, without consideration to who is involved. The high class in society will surely want to ensure that justice is not done. They will scuttle the willpower of the judiciary for their selfish ambitions. But over time, one would see that there comes a decisive power that stands to bring all offenders to book. The Bible says 'It is joy to the just to do judgment: but destruction shall be to the workers of iniquity' – Proverbs 21:15. Cases are held in the law court in public and sometimes published in the news. This is to help prove to the world that there was justice and fairness during the hearing. A case before a leader may be very compelling in the sense that there is every reason to act otherwise. But a decisive leader will push ahead through crocodile-infested water to pass judgement.

Such decisive acts of a leader may make him unpopular among the political class in society. How does this play out in our homes, churches and our overall physical wellbeing? Opportunity comes but once, they say. The leadership position you occupy today may not be there tomorrow. In your actions, try to be decisive, and let your actions be guided by thorough and productive investigations.

Forthrightness

This is the principle that ensures that everyone who errs is punished according to the contents of the law, which he/she is already aware of. This puts the onus on the leader to ensure that everyone is acquainted with the law. How would a leader gets his law across to the people he leads so that whenever anyone errs, the terms of the written and signed law will be executed? Let us see a sample of how this is done in Esther 3:12:

Then were the king's scribes called on the thirteenth day of the first month, and there was written according to all that Haman had commanded unto the king's lieutenants, and to the governors that were over every province, and to the rulers of every people of every province according to the writing thereof, and to every people after their language; in the name of king Ahasuerus was it written, and sealed with the king's ring.

The command was written and translated into the various languages so that no one would claim ignorance of what was written. It was made available to everyone, even breaking language barriers. How can we lead effectively when we are unable to communicate our dos and don'ts to the hearts of those we lead?

Another thing a forthright leader does is to be at peace with all men, so that his judgement will not be seen as a biased one: 'Wherefore laying aside all malice, and all guile, and hypocrisies, and envies, and all evil speakings...' - 1 Peter

2:1. Since justice and fairness are about impartiality, leaders must have a clean heart towards those they lead, otherwise their judgement will be clouded with impartiality. We can be forthright when we are soaked in the word of God.

The Bible says in Ephesians 6:14: 'Stand therefore, having your loins girt about with truth, and having on the breastplate of righteousness...' This is the fear of the Lord, which is only possible when, we '... take the helmet of salvation, and the sword of the Spirit, which is the word of God.' This implies that a forthright leader is one who can administer justice because he has the Holy Spirit in him. We would also see that in Luke 12:47, the principle of forthrightness is the reason why the unlawful servant will be punished for the act of disobedience: 'And that servant, which knew his lord's will, and prepared not himself, neither did according to his will, shall be beaten with many stripes.'

Forgiveness

The word of God says: 'For if ye forgive men their trespasses, your heavenly Father will also forgive you: But if ye forgive not men their trespasses, neither will your Father forgive your trespasses' - Matthew 6:14-15. The spirit of forgiveness in a leader breeds unity among those he leads. This is the bedrock of equity. Here in the book of Ezekiel is what God says: 'Again, when I say unto the wicked, Thou shalt surely die; if he turn from his sin, and do that which is lawful and right; If the wicked restore the pledge, give again that he had robbed, walk in the statutes of life, without committing iniquity; he shall surely live, he shall not die. None of his sins that he hath committed shall be mentioned unto him: he hath done that which is lawful and right; he shall surely live.' - Ezekiel 33:14-16. This implies that when a leader who has the heart of God sees one who come to repent of his/her wrongdoing, such a leader should tamper justice with mercy and forgive.

Compassion

In a helpless situation, what will become of a leader's judgement? Will he still maintain his judicial uprightness? This is where the word 'fairness' comes into play. The world is full of sin, yet God sent in Jesus to redeem us. Jesus healed many people, Jews and Gentiles alike, and told them not to sin again, implying they were actually sinners who needed to be shown the harsh side of the law. A leader's sympathetic character will enable him to teach those he leads on how they would act so as to merit his leadership favour and kindness.

CHAPTER EIGHT

LEADERSHIP PROVISION

Companies and business establishments often win the loyalty of their employees through the provision of a conducive work environment, health care for employees and their dependants, footing their holiday travel expenses, execution of a good pension scheme, etc. Jesus' ministry did not receive much popularity from teaching, but from the acts of provision – in healing and in feeding them. In John 6:15, the crowd actually wanted to make Him king by force because they perceived Him, through His acts of provision, as the answer to all they ever needed to become physically. This is why the rich often get the support of the poor whenever they contest elections. The poor will sell their consciences and futures for a morsel of flour. Every leader should be aware that the poor are always helpless, and are in most cases not ready to put to their hearts all the leadership wisdom you may be putting forward to them. All they want to see is provision. Give something to them, and they are all yours, supporting you through the days of odds, until someone else provides what supersedes your gesture. This was why Jesus said that the poor would always be there for you to cater for (Matthew 26:11).

How then can leaders provide for those they lead without making them sell their conscience and rights? This is where you must be ready to teach them, as Jesus did when they stayed with him for three days, listening to His kingdom message (Mark 8:1-21). This was why Jesus said that the poor had the gospel preached to them,

Jesus provided for His disciples throughout the period they were with Him, and after He departed this sinful world, He begged the father to release the Holy Spirit upon them to aid them in carrying out the task of rescuing this world back to what God had created.

Before we continue with this subject of provision, I would want us to read through Isaiah 55:1-4:

Ho, every one that thirsteth, come ye to the waters, and he that hath no money; come ye, buy, and eat; yea, come, buy wine and milk without money and without price. Wherefore do ye spend money for that which is not bread? and your labour for that which satisfieth not? hearken diligently unto me, and eat ye that which is good, and let your soul delight itself in fatness. Incline your ear, and come unto me: hear, and your soul shall live; and I will make an everlasting covenant with you, even the sure mercies of David. Behold, I have given him for a witness to the people, a leader and commander to the people.

Taking to heart these verses, which actually refer to the prophecy about Jesus' ministry of restoration, we would understand what God sees as provision. In verse 2 above, the Bible says: 'Wherefore do ye spend money for that which is not bread? and your labour for that which satisfieth not?' This implies that a leader's act of provision should be judged as that which would bring spiritual and physical satisfaction. In verse 4, we are informed that the one who would champion this course is a leader and commander to the people.

The following are what we often regard as leadership provision:

- Teaching/training
- Healing
- Defence
- Guidance
- Shelter
- Food
- Social amenities etc.

A thorough look at the terms of the verses will actually narrow it down to teaching/training. Every successful organisation spends enough resources in developing the intellectual instinct of its employees. If you want to be successful as a leader, be ready to educate the minds of those you lead until they agree with the vision you are driving. It takes a continuous drip of water to make the mighty ocean.

While doing this, provide what would help their physical needs, so that you can get their emotional focus. To me, there is a difference between someone who is focused and someone who is emotionally focused. Those who are emotionally focused will give their whole lives to your ideas of leadership. These we refer to as followers. These followers are like your clones that will end up living the life they see in you, the life you preached, lived and will die for. Jesus had clones who did greater things, and today more Jesus clones are been raised by God – even from stones (Luke 19:40).

As a leader, your provision should be to your followers and not to the mockers, who will only look for avenues to mock you the more. If you end up spending all your time teaching mockers assured of failure in your attempt to lead: 'Now therefore be ye not mockers, lest your bands be made strong: for I have heard from the Lord God of hosts a consumption, even determined upon the whole earth. Give ye ear, and hear my voice; hearken, and hear my speech.' - Isaiah 28:22-23.

Mockers don't like those who instruct them to live up to expectations (Proverbs 15:12). A leader knows those who are loyal to his vision. These are the ones he should spend resources on in provision.

Now let's see the story of Jacob and Esau in the Bible. Jacob didn't act as a leader. A leader provides for the need of those he leads. Until his father blessed him, he was still a primitive follower, who only saw using what he had as a means to strip others naked. Many leaders, even in the house of God, do this. Jacob only became a leader after his father blessed him. This is why we will not become successful providers until we are anointed by God.

Why should leaders see themselves as providers? This illustration will explain it better. When I was a kid and went fetching mango fruits, one person climbed the tree while others waited under to catch whatever fruit the one on the tree threw down. As long as the person up the tree kept throwing down the fruit, no one tried to throw a stone at the fruit on the tree. If however, he/she stopped throwing, those watching him from the ground picked up wood or even stones to start knocking down the fruits themselves, and the one up the tree could get hurt. A leader who does not provide for his/her followers will certainly be hurt as they try to get results unguided. This is an instance of leadership provision in the Bible: *And ye shall take one prince of every tribe, to divide the land by inheritance.* - Numbers 34:18

A leader knows his/her jurisdiction, those he must attend to their needs – for example: *But Joshua the son of Nun, which standeth before thee, he shall go in thither: encourage him: for he shall cause Israel to inherit it.* - Deuteronomy 1:38

God is our example, and he is our almighty provider. To some He provided streams, others had lakes, some had oases, while some lived on the coast. All these sources provided water. Those staying close to the sea produced salt from their water. Water gushed from the rocks to quench the taste of others. To everybody, God had provided water for their use.

Now let us see below what King Hezekiah did as a display of his leadership. I am recounting the acts of Hezekiah as a leader because the Bible says he did what was right in the sight of God (2 Chronicles 29:2). The following were his acts of leadership which made him acceptable to God:

1. He opened the house of the Lord and repaired them in order to provide a place of worship and sacrifice unto God within the first year of his reign – 2 Chronicles 29:3.

2. He recognised the importance of the Levites. He gathered them and encouraged them to sanctify the house of the Lord, thus keeping them busy and dedicated to their call of duty. This is what dynamic leaders do. He created employment and reduces the amount of idleness in society - 2 Chronicles 29:4-5.

3. He opened their understanding into why the old leaders had failed and the implication of their deeds and how it had affected the development of the people and the nation of Israel - 2 Chronicles 29:6-9.

4. He had a vision that would bring peace and tranquillity to those he led - 2 Chronicles 29:10-11.

5. The Levites obeyed him according to his order and they stationed themselves to serve, even with musical instruments, in the house of God, because the King had created the enabling environment for them to thrive - 2 Chronicles 29:15-26.

6. By commanding the Levites to sacrifice unto the Lord, he provided intercession on behalf of the nation - 2 Chronicles 29:27.

7. All the people worshipped God in an atmosphere that boasted of the presence of God, consecrating themselves before the Lord, because they had a leader that feared God. And this act will bring the peace and favour of God upon them. When leaders take the hearts of those they lead to God he has provided peace unknowingly for them - 2 Chronicles 29:28-30.

8. He encouraged the people to give sacrifices and thanksgiving offerings unto the Lord, and they responded because they had a leader who could draw them close to God. This is the height of leadership provision – reuniting them to their creator. A leader who would reunite God's children back to Him would have little worry because all the people he led would be out there praying for his success. The joy explained in 2 Chronicles 29:36, 30:26, shows how the people had expected a leader who would provide the enabling environment for them to experience peace - 2 Chronicles 29:31-36.

9. He ensured that the Passover was kept in the prescribed manner, as ordered by God. This is another point that actually moved my heart. This is where he reinvigorated the spirit of service in the hearts of the people. The Bible says: 'that they should come to keep the Passover to the Lord God of Israel at Jerusalem, since they had not done it for a long time in the prescribed manner.' – 2 Chronicles 30:5. How many leaders are ready to go against the crowd to ensure that practices are done in line with instituted order that would please God, without trying to please people to the detriment of their godly faith? Here he provided orderliness, wholesomeness and perfection.

10. He prayed for everyone, including those who had not sanctified themselves because he had the welfare of the people at heart – 2 Chronicles 30:18-20. Verse 20 says that the Lord listened to the voice of Hezekiah and healed the people, buttressing the fact I explained earlier that the people will surely prosper.

11. He encouraged the transfer of the good knowledge of the Lord through teaching by the Levites – 2 Chronicles 30:22. If our political leaders would encourage the churches to teach the undiluted word of the Lord, there would be no evil in society. But the belief that people can worship any manner of god, all in the name of freedom of association, will not bear fruits of peace, progress and unity. A leader must be firm to ensure there is effective transfer of knowledge, even in our industries. This is why I talked about training earlier.

12. In imitating the king's action in verse 20, the priests and the Levites also prayed for everyone, and God answered them as recorded in verse 27. When people begin to emulate the good gestures of the leader, there would be a multiplying effect in the nature of peace and blessings that the people will experience.

13. Apart from leading the people to God, he also provided water for his people through a tunnel that would convey water from a dam system - 2 Chronicles 32:30.

These are great provisions, and indeed the Lord made him prosper because he did all these with his heart, not waiting for man to appreciate him, but he did all with the fear of God in his heart.

Provision is related to needs, and everyone's need is different and should be met in different ways. A provision that does not meet the needs of the people we lead will never bring joy into their hearts. This is why the leadership provisions above will create the environment for prosperity to thrive in the lives of the people.

Leaders would definitely provide effectively if they would see themselves as providers. The people you lead are helpless and are looking up to you to provide for them. If you can see them as people who have one form of disability or the other, then you will be able to become the solution to their problems. Here you must get the rich to make donations to support your drive for welfare service. Jesus had dinner prepared by the rich in their homes and would go there with His disciples, who would have not been able to get such treatment from the rich. As a pastor, one of your responsibilities is to affect those in power, and to ensure that they spend the resources effectively to cater for the needs of the poor in society, and then the provision of social amenities. What many pastors have done is to seek money from those in seats of governance to build their cathedrals, and buy expensive cars with money from government officials. These are not leaders, they are tyrants. A leader is more of a wealth-balancing machine. He gets money from the rich, and creates a favourable environment for both the rich and the poor to thrive together as one family.

CHAPTER NINE

LEADERSHIP DEFENCE

Jesus made Himself available when they came to arrest Him to die for our sins, setting His disciples free: 'Jesus answered, I have told you that I am he: if therefore ye seek me, let these go their way' - John 18:8. He volunteered to die for our sins. He is our advocate before God. A good shepherd defends his sheep. One way He does this is by equipping them with knowledge ahead of time, so they are not led astray. A leader must be ready to defend those he/she leads. Interceding on behalf of those you lead is active defence. Let's see how Moses prayed for defence:

I prayed therefore unto the Lord, and said, O Lord God, destroy not thy people and thine inheritance, which thou hast redeemed through thy greatness, which thou hast brought forth out of Egypt with a mighty hand. Remember thy servants, Abraham, Isaac, and Jacob; look not unto the stubbornness of this people, nor to their wickedness, nor to their sin: Lest the land whence thou broughtest us out say, Because the Lord was not able to bring them into the land which he promised them, and because he hated them, he hath brought them out to slay them in the wilderness. Yet they are thy people and thine inheritance, which thou broughtest out by thy mighty power and by thy stretched out arm. Deuteronomy 9:26-29

Jesus told God that He had equipped His disciples with all the information that God has given to Him (John 17:6). And He also made them to be aware of the fact that they had been made clean by the word they had received from Him, making them know the importance of the word of God in their lives – that if they would indeed know the word of God by heart, they would experience proactive defence against the manipulations of the devil. This is required so that they can become wise, and be able to survive in the midst of wolves. He had earlier taught His disciples that the children of this world are wiser. This is the same reason Moses had to teach the children of Israel that the favour they were getting was not because they were perfect. Defence is likened to the act of leadership intercession through prayers.

I would classify defence into passive and active. Feeding your followers with knowledge is active defence. Interceding on their behalf when they go wrong to ensure they are not punished by God is passive defence. I see it as passive because they may not even know where they went wrong, and so the defence they are experiencing is as a result of the leader's active relationship with God, or with the supreme human authority that is available in organisational hierarchy.

But this should not be the case always. People need to be knowledgeable about the status and codes and the available rules, which are operative within that circle. Moses disobeyed God because the people He was leading never had an active relationship with God, due to the simple fact that they had someone who they felt would always intercede for them.

A leader should be able to equip His followers with the knowledge that can safeguard them from satanic assault. This is what Christ meant when He said we should be as wise as a serpent. Ephesians 6:12 taught us that we are in a spiritual wrestling battle. This battle is knowledge based. We can deduce this from how Jesus destabilised Satan when He was tempted by him.

Moses equipped the children of Israel with knowledge of what they should do when they see opposition in Deuteronomy 20:1-3:

When you go out to battle against your enemies, and see horses and chariots and people more numerous than you, do not be afraid of them; for the Lord your God is with you, who brought you up from the land of Egypt. So it shall be, when you are on the verge of battle, that the priest shall approach and speak to the people. And he shall say to them, 'Hear, O Israel: Today you are on the verge of battle with your enemies. Do not let your heart faint, do not be afraid, and do not tremble or be terrified because of them.'

The entire chapter is more of an empowerment lecture

that tells them what to do at every given time and situation. This lecture will definitely give them the boldness to overcome their fears of extermination. A leader should be ready to make those he leads know that he depends on the power of God to see them through.

We know that God is a defender, so everyone who would look up to Him will surely be defended against enemy plots. This should be a leader's quest daily, preparing the hearts of his followers against the attacks of the wolves which come from the enemies to your vision in the form of mockery, curses, rebellion, sowing seeds of discord, ingratitude, etc. When Jesus sent out the disciples, He also let them know that some people would indeed reject the gospel, so that it wouldn't come to them as a surprise, thereby discouraging them from moving forward. A leader who feeds those who look up to him with the kind of knowledge that make them defensive in the midst of chaos is a leader with the heart of posterity.

Many of us cannot pray because we lack the knowledge that can lead us through the prayer cycle. Many of us die in our ignorance and pride because we are empty. The disciples of Jesus knew the importance of this, and they asked Jesus to teach them how to pray. And later Jesus taught them that they must seek before they can find and that they have to ask before they can receive. To me, active defence is all we need to become free. Jesus said we shall know the truth. This is all we need. Interceding is fruitful when it can release the recipient from sin or destruction forever. If we keep on interceding passively, we may end up not leading a single soul to God. Jesus knew the importance of this when he was always telling people to sin no more after healing them. They were healed because of the relationship Jesus had with God, but that healing needed to be permanent if they were to keep away from sin.

If we look at Jesus' pattern of leadership, we see the transfer of wisdom to His disciples. We are told in Deuteronomy 34:9 that Moses transferred the spirit of wisdom upon Joshua. This is how a leader defends those he leads. He brings them in contact with knowledge, and teaches them how to seek it, understand it and imbibe the ideas contained in it.

The defence of leadership vision against the destructive hands of the enemy is only possible when a leader is watched by God. This implies that the vision you are driving must have to do with God's overall goal of putting smiles on the faces of His children. This is why setting up an entrepreneurial outfit for the sake of employing God's children so that they don't go hungry and complain against Him will receive the blessings of God. In the book of 2 Kings 19:34, God says: 'For I will defend this city, to save it for My own sake and for My servant David's sake.'

There are two reasons given above why God says His

defence presence will be felt – for His name's sake, because Jerusalem is dedicated to Him, and for the sake of David who, dedicated Jerusalem to Him by making sure his son Solomon had what it would take to raised a magnificent temple to honour God before his death (1 Chronicles 29). If the vision you are driving is dedicated to God and your heart is sanctified to live for Him, you will see His defensive presence in your vision. As a leader, your drive is to ensure that God is leading you so that you don't lead others astray. It should be a concern to you that you can lead an entire nation into pain by not submitting unto the Lord, and causing those you lead to do likewise.

Leaders could also use the presence of law enforcement agents like the police to create an atmosphere of physical defence in the heart of those they lead, and then the vision they drive as the police or security agents mount the gates and entrance to office areas. This is why nations all over the world have their own defence forces, and companies have the physical presence of security agents.

CHAPTER TEN

LEADERSHIP ESTABLISHMENT

Once a leader drives his vision with passion, he becomes emotionally focused. This was what Christ implied when He said that where our treasure is, there also will our heart be (Luke 12:34). The heart He refers to here is more of a 'passionate appeal of intent.' Our intentions are glued to our hearts' desires. As leaders, when our hearts' desires lack long-term purpose, there is no way we can become established. Your wise sayings and advices will never hit the rock or fall on deaf ears as an established leader. Once those you lead can recite your wise sayings by heart, establishment is coming your way. Once they can learn the mission and vision statement by heart, you should know that the vision you are driving will not die with your demise. Establishment comes with imbibing your own school of thought, which they that follow you have seen to work in their lives.

Leaders should think daily how they can become established in their calling. Jesus Christ is an established leader, hence He called Himself the 'true vine' (John 15:1). And He taught us that to become established in our thoughts and actions, we must follow Him (John 15:5). Samuel was established because he walked with the authority of God: 'And all Israel from Dan even to Beersheba knew that Samuel was established to be a prophet of the Lord. And the Lord appeared again in Shiloh: for the Lord revealed himself to Samuel in Shiloh by the word of the Lord.' - 1 Samuel 3:20-21. His establishment came after the Lord had revealed Himself to Samuel – this is wisdom.

How was Samuel established? The only knowledge he knew was God, because he grew as a child in God's house. The only wisdom he ever knew was the duty to serve God. Therefore there would be no evil communication coming out of him. From this portion we just read in the Bible, we would see that Samuel's establishment as a true leader of the people was based on the revelations he had from God, which were facts that no one would deny as true because they would see the hand of God in action, putting what he had revealed to pass. And we would say that because his thoughts were filled with the wisdom of God, he became established.

The Bible says again in Proverbs 16:3: 'Commit thy works unto the Lord, and thy thoughts shall be established'. This means that a leader must be ready to submit to the leadership and tutelage of God, ensuring that he does nothing outside what God approves of him/her (John 15:6-10). God is looking for those whose necks He can bend to look only in the direction He wants. Hence He complained that the children of Israel were stiff-necked (Exodus 32:9); and their establishment became impossible until 40 years of wandering in the wilderness. A leader who operates with an established thought is one with God. There is no arguing that God is an established creator of the universe and all that dwells in it. For instance, in Genesis 8:22, God says: "As long as the earth endures, seedtime and harvest, cold and heat, summer and winter, day and night will never cease."(NIV) And we could see that, indeed, the world has responded to this decree from God till date.

Establishment can only happen when we are humble, because there is no maturity without learning. This is the reason behind the Bible saying that Moses was most humble before his days, in his days and beyond his days. One would see why God had to make him the first to begin recording a historic fact now found in the Bible – the Pentateuch; Genesis, Exodus, Leviticus, Numbers, and Deuteronomy. All established leaders live in people's hearts. The Jews were ready to stone anyone to death in defence of the laws of Moses. That is what establishment does. I have seen leaders whose followers were willing to throw them out of power when they erred. Moses erred against God by defying His instruction to speak to the rock of Meribah (Numbers 20:10-13), yet he is still celebrated.

We should now be asking ourselves - if we find ourselves in Moses' situation, will those we lead carry on with our vision? Some may argue here that the vision Moses was bearing was God's own vision. Yes, it was God's own vision of restoration, but God told Moses whose vision it was. The Bible says: 'And the Lord said to Moses, 'Go, get down! For your people whom you brought out of the land of Egypt have corrupted themselves. They have turned aside quickly out of the way which I commanded them.' - Exodus 32:7-8.

We should not forget in a hurry that Moses actually started this rescue mission without God telling him to: 'Now it came to pass in those days, when Moses was grown, that he went out to his brethren and looked at their burdens. And he saw an Egyptian beating a Hebrew, one of his brethren. So he looked this way and that way, and when he saw no one, he killed the Egyptian and hid him in the sand.' - Exodus 2:11-12

This further supports the fact that leaders become established when they do what their heart yearns for. Moses' heart yearned for deliverance, and God called him to deliver His children from bondage. This is why Proverbs 16:3 referred to our thoughts being established by God. So it is all about your thoughts. What are you thinking right now? What you think is what you believe, because 'As a man thinketh in his heart, so is he...' (Proverbs 23:7). What you are thinking right now is fused with the vision you are driving. And if what occupies your mind is more about perishable possessions, then you are not yet a leader.

This is where many acclaimed leaders miss the point. Their thoughts are worthless – filled with evil manipulations. Once a leader is established, then he or she grows more branches and becomes like a giant tree, providing shelter to everything underneath. This is also where many go wrong, because they deny the little trees growing underneath the full rays of the sun which they need for photosynthesis. We should be more protective and less selfish when we carry everyone along. This is the power of the anointing of God – it takes you through the stages of spiritual, emotional, and physical wellbeing.

Psalm 89:20, tells us that it is the anointing of the Lord that establishes a leader: 'I have found My servant David; With My holy oil I have anointed him, With whom My hand shall be established; Also My arm shall strengthen him.'

Before we leave this chapter, I want to take us through a process of establishment, which I see to be an ordered path of God because of what He is doing in my life. When I got this calling, little did I know what God's call was all about, because I was not the kind of Christian one would expect – I hardly attended Sunday church services. In Isaiah 42:16, God told me that I have to walk with Him on a path that He alone would lead me on. Today I am becoming more conversant with this path of righteousness: 'He restores my soul; He leads me in the paths of righteousness For His name's sake.' - Psalms 23:3. This implies further that the only way a leader will become established is when God restores his/her soul from destruction. We would at this juncture go through the process of leadership establishment:

- A leader gets in touch with God to drive a vision for Him which becomes more of an assigned responsibility which people see as your destiny – this is what I often term 'the main anointing.'

- In the fullness of time, the growing leader informs others of the vision and starts making them see the vision through his actions. Here he acts more like a servant to those he is taking through the process of vision maturation.

- A time comes when he/she begins to see that those people he/she is explaining the vision to have actually start acting it. This is where he/she has actually become a leader.

- Gradually those he leads start leading smaller units, helping them to mature the vision. Here he/she is more of a supervisory leader or an overseer. He/she demands reports periodically to ensure that the vision is maturing.

- He/she goes back to God more often now, to ensure he/she is still within the track and destination path agreed with God.

We can extract this pattern to mature whatever vision we are driving in life.

CHAPTER ELEVEN

LEADERSHIP EXPLOITS

Every leader should see himself or herself reaching out to a multitude. Even in business, they should see themselves as solving the problems of a large number of people. We would be starting this with what the Bible judges as God's expectations of leaders as it relates to territorial largeness and increase.

John the Baptist taught us that the government of Jesus will increase. This is evidence that God loves increase. In Genesis chapter 1, we find that God could have easily left the world in the chaotic form it was, but His love for increase is the singular reason He had to intervene so as to rescue the world from deadness. Every leader with the heart of God thinks how they would expand the territorial boundaries of their influence on those they lead. Jesus even wished that His disciples should do greater things than He did. This is how leaders should feel about the vision they are driving. I am not comfortable when leaders tend to be satisfied with exacting little influence.

We are told that the earth and its fullness belong to God. The fullness of this earth is innumerable, yet the Bible talks about the secret things God is still withholding from us (Deuteronomy 29:29). This last fact takes us to what I will call leadership 'top secrets'. Those secrets are what lead to a leader's territorial increase, and they bring increase when they are revealed to those who walk and work with the leader. Later we will see how a leader can sustain growth in the vision he drives as he carefully harbours the secrets of largeness and increase in his heart.

David's large heart enabled him to build the city of David. He further saved much so that his son Solomon would be able to build the temple of God. A leader thinks increase always. John the Baptist said that the government of Jesus would increase. The leader must have the heart of ambition. The prayer of Jabez points to exploits.

Exploits are about growing your ambition as a leader in the following ways:

- Sowing the seed of territorial largeness and increase is the first thing every leader must do. This may start with you making statements of dissatisfaction about what you see around you or in the life you are living. You may see my book *How Good and Large is your Land?* for an understanding of this process.

- Securing the secrets in your heart may take you a lifetime, because God is not in a hurry to reveal. He does this in a stepwise order, depending on the questions that fill your thoughts.

- Maturing them in your thoughts as a leader is the next thing that comes to your heart, because of the awareness you are getting from the wisdom that now fills your heart. You study more this period and you may start writing it down. This was what led to what you find in the pages of the Bible you may be holding in your hand right now, and even this book you are reading. What I write are answers from the Lord to the questions I ask Him daily. He speaks and I write, so that I take the position of a secretary who takes down the minutes of meetings.

- Coin these enlargement secrets into mission and vision statements in such a way that the secrets are revealed in coded form, making the secret more of a top secret. Draw up your article of faith with your main focus on the important aspects of the top secrets. Generate the vision beliefs, policies, rules, regulations, laws, codes of conduct, etc to ensure that the coded secrets have become operational in the hearts of whoever imbibes the codes, because they are now in forms that they can easily learn by rote.

- Living them every day of your life – reciting the article of faith, the policies, and every other coinage from the secrets of the vision you are driving.

- Reveal them bit by bit in your training sections or in books aimed at turning the hearts of those you lead to accept the vision you are driving as a way of life, yet in a seemingly coded form.

- Watch them live it and don't hesitate to punish those who err. In the same way, reward those who are fervent and dedicated to the course of the vision.

- Mature it in their hearts through repetitive training. This is important if you want them to grow to become your vision bearers. Joshua only did as Moses instructed him. He bore the vision in his heart and successfully led the Israelites into the land of Canaan, yet the song of Moses as their leader never stopped resounding in their mouths. Today no believer will say anything without the thought of Christ in his/her heart. This is because Christ matured the vision in the hearts of His disciples before His death. And when He was resurrected, He continued to open up top secrets to them. Today we see the effect of His ministry and vision.

- Expect territorial largeness and increase as your subordinates now live it by and large, wherever they go.

CHAPTER TWELVE

LEADERSHIP LOYALTY

As a leader you must know to whom your loyalty is due. This is where many leaders fail. Before we continue with this discussion on how a leader can submit to God and make the people he leads believe that he does, let us take a look at an instance in the Bible of what the people's desire is, as it relates to how to uphold their service to God and why they love their God:

And Jehoshaphat stood in the congregation of Judah and Jerusalem, in the house of the Lord, before the new court, And said, O Lord God of our fathers, art not thou God in heaven? and rulest not thou over all the kingdoms of the heathen? and in thine hand is there not power and might, so that none is able to withstand thee? Art not thou our God, who didst drive out the inhabitants of this land before thy people Israel, and gavest it to the seed of Abraham thy friend forever? And they dwelt therein, and have built thee a sanctuary therein for thy name, saying, If, when evil cometh upon us, as the sword, judgment, or pestilence, or famine, we stand before this house, and in thy presence, (for thy name is in this house,) and cry unto thee in our affliction, then thou wilt hear and help. - 2 Chronicles 20: 5-9.

Now let us look at the verses of the Bible above; the people gathered as a congregation in the house of God, seemingly afraid of their enemies, in the sanctuary which they had built for God for the purpose of having a place where they would render their hearts before God, seeking for His hand of deliverance, so that they would experience freedom. What else is the responsibility of a leader if not to make those he leads experience freedom? A leader who wants to live in the hearts of the people must be ready to build a worship centre for them. They will easily see you as one identifying with their course when you do this. People love God and want to serve Him, so any leader who sacrifices in building a house of worship and fellowship unto God is bound to succeed. The people see this act by leaders as a show of Love:

And a certain centurion's servant, who was dear to him, was sick and ready to die. So when he heard about Jesus, he sent elders of the Jews to Him, pleading with Him to come and heal his servant. And when they came to Jesus, they begged Him earnestly, saying that the one for whom He should do this was deserving, 'for he loves our nation, and has built us a synagogue.' Then Jesus went with them...' - Luke 7:2-6

From the story above, it would be considered that the centurion lived in the hearts of the Jews because he built a place of worship for them. And that singular act qualified him as one who deserved the help of God even when he was not in the Mosaic covenant.

Submitting to the authority of God, who has made it possible for you to lead, is very important to the success of the vision you are driving. The show of submission to God can easily be interpreted by those you lead through your acts. Noah built an ark as God instructed, and then sacrificed unto God. Nimrod failed as a leader when he led the building of the tower of Babel with reasons against God's command to fill and subdue the earth. Abraham raised altars for God wherever he went in order to call upon the name of God. Isaac and his son, Jacob, continued this act of altar worship. Moses built the tabernacle in the wilderness, and institutionalised the Jewish worship order. King David saved to build God's temple and his son, Solomon, laid the foundation and completed the project. Nehemiah built the wall of Jerusalem, while Zerubbabel rebuilt the temple after it was destroyed by the Babylonian king. To tell us how the Jews valued the temple Solomon built, we could see how they hated Jesus when He told them that He will rebuild the temple in three days (John 2:19-20).

Now, our submission to God as leaders has a lot to do with hearing and acting on the instructions of God. Moses failed the moment he omitted to carry out God's instruction. In

Exodus 23:20, God made mention of leading us with His angel. Anybody leading God's children is under the influence of a leading angel. Now, which angel is leading us? Is it the angel of light or the angel of darkness? A righteous leader, who leads with the fear of God in his/her heart, is guided by the angel of light, and for a leader who leads with pride in his/her heart; we also know that he/she leads under the instruction of the angel of darkness – the devil.

In Luke 22:42, Jesus says: 'Father, if thou be willing, remove this cup from me: nevertheless not my will, but thine, be done.' Jesus' submission to the will of God by dying for our sins is a clear sign that we all need to yield to the leadership and guidance of God. This is what will make us become effective leaders, and those we lead will be obliged to follow us down the stormy path of leadership. And at the end, we will see the light of God shining on our paths, and the vision will receive illumination from the throne of heaven, reflecting values of dedication from the hearts of those under your leadership canopy.

I will advise you to build for God if you want to succeed as a leader – either as a husband, father, wife, mother, governor, president, general manager – you name it. You must be ready to enter into the hearts of the people you lead as a live image that never fades, and this you can easily do by building a house of worship for them. They will support your vision of restoration if you can keep them busy in the house of God, because this is the whole duty of man: 'Let us hear the conclusion of the whole matter: Fear God, and keep his commandments: for this is the whole duty of man. For God shall bring every work into judgment, with every secret thing, whether it be good, or whether it be evil.' - Ecclesiastes 12:13-14.

As a leader, you must know that your loyalty is to God, all the time.

CHAPTER THIRTEEN

LEADERSHIP SERVICE

Not until we submit unto God will we be able to serve humanity. In the Article of Faith of the Royal Diamonds International Church (aka Christ Movement), which we will be looking into soon, one would see this service clearly demonstrated which sends a message to whoever is reading it that the church stands for service to God and Humanity:

1. GOD the holy
2. GOD the righteous
3. GOD the faithful
4. GOD the omnipresent
5. GOD that showeth compassion
6. GOD the merciful
7. OUR joyful GOD
8. GOD our inheritance
9. GOD the supernatural
10. GOD the unstoppable
11. GOD the mover

12. GOD the igniter

13. GOD that subdues our enemies

14. We worship you

15. We adore you

16. We honour you

17. We give you praise

18. Use us as your instruments

19. We believe that you sent your only son Jesus Christ to die for our sins

20. We are ever willing to carry out your instructions

21. We pray, prepare us for this glorious task

22. That all men shall come to know you as GOD

23. We pray, have mercy upon us

24. Let your healing power dwell in us

25. Take us with your right hand and lead us

26. We understand that your calling is not with repentance

27. But this we ask of you

28. That we may be found worthy of your holy name

29. That our life shall testify of your glory

30. In the midst of our imperfection, use us

31. In the midst of our ignorance, lead us

32. In the midst of temptations, teach us

33. So that we can stand tall in the midst of our enemies

34. To proclaim your amazing works in our life

35. This is our desire - as we totally surrender to your will

36. In JESUS NAME - AMEN.

Earlier we talked about coining your leadership top secret in a form that may be easily recited like a national anthem, so that it will live in the hearts of those you lead. A look at the article above would send a message of orderliness – 36 lines, 12 times 3. This is a spiritual perfect order respected in the Bible from the 12 tribes of Israel. One could also see it as 6 times 6, where the number 6 would represent the days of creation, when God restored the once chaotic and formless world into the form we can feel today. This understanding will quickly send to the heart of the congregation what the article represents: it is all about restoration.

Now let us look at each of the lines and what we would learn from them:

Line 1 talks of the Holiness of God. Lines 2 through 13 (12 lines) explains what the Holiness of God is all about. It is like when Jesus says in the Lord's Prayer 'Our Father who art in Heaven.' Those listening to Him would eventually look up into the sky if they would see the Father He referred to. From here, those you lead will have a perfect understanding of what your vision stands to achieve. It helps them to know who you are submitting to, and the source of the wisdom you display before them. Since your vision is an offshoot of your spiritual source of strength, they know exactly what to expect at the end of the day – this is a guide to the coded secrets that lie in your heart, because people predict the unknown from what they know presently.

Lines 14 through 17 explains how you revere God in your heart, which forms the embodiment of the life you live and believe in. From here those you are trying to lead, or sell the vision to, will be able to judge your intentions – remember that you are trying to get people and woo them to become part of the vision you are driving, so that they will work and walk with you to ensure that the vision live on, even after your death. Be mindful of this fact.

Line 18 tells those who will work with me, their responsibility to this God – as instruments of restoration. In line 19, the article reassures them who the vision is hinged upon – they know that sin burns in our hearts, but they also want to do away with sin, or whatever is weighing them down. Give them the assurance that their sins have been paid for. That they can become free is only a matter of choice – if indeed they will drive this vision with you. We can also see this in John 3:16.

As a matter of emphasis, line 20 explains the vision again. In line 21, the article explains the source of our strength, which we depend on, and it also explains the nature/reward of the vision. Line 22 defines the vision in a simple yet clear language. There is a fact that the article deals with, and that is that human beings finds it difficult to forget their pasts, and as such, their acts of sin keep weighing them down, making it difficult for them to live a new life. This is why Christ talked about the act of being born again, which is basically the act of renewing our minds with the positive events that now happen to us. This is why in lines 23 through 24, the article gives the assurance of God's mercy and the beauty of this mercy.

Lines 25 through 26 emphasise who is leading us and that He is not going to fail us. Anyone who sees this and understands it will yield his/her heart to serve. The mind of the congregation and my fellow vision bearers is refocused in line 27 through 29 to what we expect to happen to us as the light to the world. Lines 30 through 32 put across the obstacles that we may experience and reassure us that God will help us in overcoming them.

Now the last four lines end this article with the physical rewards and the name behind our success. Line 33 talks of the earthly reward waiting for the vision bearers, even in the midst of their enemies – from David's statement in Psalm 23:5: 'Thou preparest a table before me in the presence of mine enemies...' Line 34 explains the beauty of service to God, which is a paraphrase of our vision statement taken from Hebrews 12:23, explained earlier in this book. Line 35 encourages them to desire the terms of the article, which is a sum total of someone walking perfectly with God in line with our mission statement quoted earlier in this book. And line 36 refocuses our hearts and thoughts to Jesus, the author and finisher of our faith (Hebrew 12:1-2).

Anyone who understands this article of faith will be moved in his/her heart to be part of this vision.

In order to render effective service to God and humanity as a leader we will be using the 'SMART-P' principle. There is much about the S.M.A.R.T goal setting principle from which I am deriving this - Specific, Measurable, Attainable, Realistic and Time-bound goals. I have added P – Purposeful - because I have seen that while people can set these SMART goals, many leaders can hardly explain the purpose behind the goals they are setting. So I have decided to bring out the salient element in the SMART goal-setting principle, hence Purposeful.

Before we move further we should explain the letters in our SMART-P principle that will aid us in ensuring we render quality, God-fearing service to God and humanity.

S – Specific: The Bible taught us what Jesus' goal was when he commenced preaching in Matthew 4:17: From that time Jesus began to preach, and to say, Repent: for the kingdom of heaven is at hand. His mission statement can be coined from this verse. A specific objective is simple yet focused and everyone would easily have a quick understanding of what your vision stands to achieve.

M – Measurable: This is where standards come in. What is God demanding from us? Jesus gave us the yardstick God is going to use to measure our service here on earth in Matthew 5:48, where He says 'Be ye therefore perfect, even as your Father which is in heaven is perfect'. And this brings us to the next question: How can we be perfect?

This is why you are reading this book. Perfection comes through leading others into the heights of them having a perfect walk with God. As you read through this book to digest the wisdom it preaches, and uphold them, your thoughts will become refined, and will embed the elements of purity and sanctity.

A – Attainable: Jesus told us that with God, all we want to achieve is ever possible. God would not call us into a service that will prove abortive. In Exodus 3:12, He instructed Moses that upon their arrival at Mount Sinai, they should serve Him, though the Israelites murmured instead. If we would take rebellion out of our hearts, we will serve Him. There is nothing that involves service to God that is not within our reach. As a leader, what you should be planning is service geared towards a specific purpose within a specific framework. In that way you will be able to compare such service with

God's standard. Too much planned service at a time will only lead to clumsy achievements, and may lead to a lot of rework. Here again, I will want us to become emotionally focused as we serve God and humanity in our leadership pursuit.

R – Realistic: A leader must be ready to plan realistic services. Many would build skyscrapers in the air with their mouths, and will start to drive those they lead into trying to achieve 'white elephant' plans. This type of leadership will only bring unending hopes of achievement without practical results. A realistic goal leads to a realistic service. It involves realistic planning with the resources at hand, so that those you lead will believe in you always because of the results they are seeing. Too many unfulfilled promises have never augured well with people, anywhere, any time.

T – Time bound: This is how to measure performance. A leader should have fixed time for delivery of service. Recycling plans without achieving results will breed distrust in the hearts of those you lead. What the people want to see is results. Let them know what can be achieved and when. Never indulge in procrastination. Fulfil all your promises at the expected time. When you delegate actions, ensure that these are delivered at fixed times. Leadership failures all over the world are often measured in time slippages when the leader promised to deliver a promise to the people he leads.

P – Purposeful: A leader should be able to offer himself to the service he/she has been called into. The purpose of his leadership call must be live in his heart, and he must give his life for it. The purpose should be the treasure he seeks. This way, his heart will be there, helping him to carry on the service of selflessness day in day out.

Finally, we need to absorb the words of Jesus Christ below as we serve:

But it shall not be so among you: but whosoever will be great among you, let him be your minister; And whosoever will be chief among you, let him be your servant: Even as the Son of man came not to be ministered unto, but to minister, and to give his life a ransom for many. - Matthew 20:26-28.

CHAPTER FOURTEEN

MATURING THE LEADERSHIP VISION

Without vision there is no leadership; without leadership there is no vision. Isn't it wonderful to see that all the while we have been talking we have mentioned the word 'vision' more often than any other word as we discuss the tenets of leadership? This is why it is taking a chapter by itself. But before we continue, I would want us to take a pause for 30 minutes or so to ponder over what vision is really all about from what we have discussed so far.

Vision is simply seeing with a good eye. We would be taking off with our discussion from what Jesus says about the good and the evil eye:

For where your treasure is, there will your heart be also. The light of the body is the eye: if therefore thine eye be single, thy whole body shall be full of light. But if thine eye be evil, thy whole body shall be full of darkness. If therefore the light that is in thee be darkness, how great is that darkness! - Matthew 6:21-23.

As we discuss leadership vision, we can refer to the verses

above. The first verse says that there is a treasure somewhere. This is the vision you are driving as a leader. To ensure you have hold of the treasure, your heart must be there also – this is what I referred to earlier as emotional focus. Now, to keep the vision within our reach, we must see it with a single eye, meaning that what we should see in our vision must be free from corruption. Other translations called it 'good eye'. What the eyes sees is planted in the heart, from which it either pollutes or edifies the body, and this is why the Bible says it is the light of the body, wherefore it is said in that same portion we just read that the evil eye – polluted vision ‑ brings disappointments. The heart referred to here is our reasoning faculty. To this end, we would say that a successful vision is one which has a goal, simply referred to earlier as treasure, and then it must be focused on emotionally with our inward sight, thus explaining the vision in parts, in such a way that the heart is filled with the vision.

To be able to drive any vision, the leader must have answers to the five Ws and the H of the vision he is conceiving in his heart. These are the Why, Where, When, What, Who, and How. For instance, let's take a look at the message of God to Moses before he went ahead to bring the children of Israel from the land of Egypt:

And the Lord said, I have surely seen the affliction of my people which are in Egypt, and have heard their cry by reason of their taskmasters; for I know their sorrows; And I am come down to deliver them out of the hand of the Egyptians, and to bring them up out of that land unto a good land and a large, unto a land flowing with milk and honey; unto the place of the Canaanites, and the Hittites, and the Amorites, and the Perizzites, and the Hivites, and the Jebusites. Now therefore, behold, the cry of the children of Israel is come unto me: and I have also seen the oppression wherewith the Egyptians oppress them. Come now therefore, and I will send thee unto Pharaoh, that thou mayest bring forth my people the children of Israel out of Egypt. – Exodus 3:7-10

Moses' vision was simply to bring the children of Israel out of Egypt, as seen in the last verse above. The statement didn't say that Moses would eventually take them into the Promised Land. God's own responsibility, which would be seen as His vision for the children of Israel at that material time can be seen in the second statement - verse 8: 'And I am come down to deliver them...' Many often feel bad that God couldn't allow Moses to enter the land because of the disrespect he unintentionally showed for God in Numbers 20, but they obviously fail to see what Exodus 3:10 says about Moses' own responsibility.

After Moses received this vision of deliverance from God, He started asking questions to find a definite explanation of the five Ws and H of the vision he was about to drive. We see later, in the book of Exodus, how he went up to seek the face of God in the mountain, and later came back with the Ten Commandments. From the Exodus verses 3:7-10 we just read, we can see how the five Ws and H turns out:

- Why: 'And the Lord said, I have surely seen the affliction of my people which are in Egypt, and have heard their cry by reason of their taskmasters; for I know their sorrows'.

- Where: From the land of sorrow, Egypt on to the land of prosperity, Canaanites, and the Hittites, and the Amorites, and the Perizzites, and the Hivites, and the Jebusites.

- When: Now! – no further delay. This very moment is the right time to deliver them as He couldn't bear the sorrows of their hearts any longer.

- What: Deliverance: 'that thou mayest bring forth my people'.

- Who: God, Moses, and the Israelites.

- How: 'Come now therefore, and I will send thee unto Pharaoh'.

One would ask why did God decide to send Moses to Pharaoh. He could have as well blindfolded the Egyptians and led His children out and when they were out, He would open their eyes, but God chose to raise a leader to bring them out. Again, if we look into the Abraham's vision which God also gave to him in Genesis 12:1-3, we would also see the five Ws and H clearly spelt out:

- Why: Abram was about to be blessed by God – from Abram (exalted father) to Abraham (father of a nation)
- Where: From Ur, land of poverty, to a land God would show him where he would experience prosperity.
- When: Now! The moment God was through with talking with him.
- What: Deliverance and restoration: Blessings, relationship with God and relocation.
- Who: God and Abraham
- How: Obeying God and stepping out of his home in a walk with God. You will remember that earlier on we discussed what I termed 'leadership step out.'

The vision we have is what energises our inward mind to move out of our present state. It is more of an impulse stimulus. Once the vision is defined, there is no way our minds can be at rest until we fulfil the terms that will lead to the actualisation of the vision. Now, let us also look at John 3:16 and bring out the five Ws and H in that eternal vision of restoration:

- Why: For God so loved the world...
- Where: The world.
- When: Now! In the present.... still active in our present generation.

- What: Deliverance and restoration.
- Who: God, His son Jesus Christ and the world (Including you and me).
- How: Jesus died for our sins. We have to believe in Jesus to be saved from eternal death.

As an aspiring successful leader, design a logo to represent the vision you are about to drive. Create a flag to explain the vision. Create an image that represents what the vision stands for. Moses' brazen serpent and the cross of Jesus are images that represent the vision of deliverance and restoration. These all will speak the vision and plant it in the hearts of those you lead. This is why God always makes covenants with His chosen servants. John 3:16 is a fulfilment of a typical covenant of promise in Isaiah 42:16.

Before we discuss how a leader could mature his vision, let us also take a look at the Vision Statement of the Royal Diamonds International Church: To be the general assembly and church of the firstborn which is written in heaven (Hebrew 12:22-24) – The Church that Overcometh (Revelations 3:5).

- Why: To make heaven.
- Where: Heaven.
- When: Whenever it pleases God – meaning that we must be fully prepared to make heaven at all times.

- What: To overcome temptations for the sake of making heaven.
- Who: Everyone in our fold referred to here as the church.
- How: By overcoming the temptations of the devil.

The Mission Statement of the church actually explored the 'How and What' better: To Recruit, Train and Spiritually empower men, women, youths and children with the wisdom to execute the will of God on Earth.

From our discussion above, we can say that a vision starts with an apparent obstacle that would hinder your progress in life and you are finding a clue to what to do to enable you to walk out of your present chaotic situation. Here many would want to submit to a vision already being driving by a leader so as to experience the kind of life they desire, and gradually they would learn about the vision on-the-job and may grow to become a leader there, or some would finally develop their vision and move out to start driving theirs. In the church, this is what many refer to as breakout.

Getting a job in an establishment is one way you could learn to develop your vision in life. I have seen many companies flourishing today because the owners were once employees in a similar company. Now visions need to be explained in clear language. On one occasion Jesus used the statement (Matthew 16:18): 'And I say also unto thee, That thou art Peter, and upon this rock I will build my church; and the gates of hell shall not prevail against it.' Here the disciples knows immediately that all Jesus was doing was to build a church that would stand the test of eternity, where the church would be filled with divine wisdom to enable it thrive in the midst of temptations from the devil. So they would know that they were in for a job of restoration.

Every vision is out to surmount an obstacle to progress. In Exodus 3:3 God only spoke to Moses when he had decided to turn aside and see the burning bush, meaning that not until we are ready to confront the shock in our lives and know its source will we receive the vision to get into our announcement in life.

Below I have outlined a few steps that could lead to vision maturation:

- You have a problem at hand. Maybe it is a general societal concern that is being discussed in all corners. There is mass dissatisfaction everywhere. Even the church is not left out – doctrinal challenges are derailing the populace. It could also be that the standard of a particular product you have is not satisfactory to you. You have also seen the reason to join in the complaint. This is how vision starts. Your next concern would be how to provide a solution to the ailing situation that you could easily define. Exodus 2:25 explains that God, indeed, acknowledged the suffering of the children of Israel – this is the reason why He had to intervene.

- It is time to see with your good eye, as explained earlier. You filter the odds and define the gains from the odds if they are attended to as God did to the earth when it was experiencing deformation. Abraham lifted up his eyes and saw the days of Jesus, about 2000 years ahead of him. But before this could happen, he faced the challenge of survival as Lot; his nephew had chosen the best part of the land (Genesis 13:7-16). He was left with nothing, so to say. But after God spoke to him, we are told that Abraham saw his vision (vs. 15) and moved to claim it as he responded to God's instruction to walk through the length and breadth of the land (vs. 17). We would see how he established the vision in the heart of God by raising an altar to mark the event in vs. 18. This is what seeing with your good eyes is all about. It shows that you know your source of triumph, you make Him part of the vision.

- It is time to start the process of self-discovery. Here you will begin to know what you need to put together to clearly define the terms of the vision. Jacob had to wear Esau's clothes to fit in as one who Isaac would eventually bless (Genesis 27:11). You seek more knowledge here. You may be reading and digesting so many books relating to the vision you are about to drive. This is why you should also enrol in a course in the university or any higher institution of study. And while you are there searching for knowledge, you a framing your vision statement and mission statement. A read through Exodus chapter 3 would explain this stage of the vision maturation process.

- You have finally stumbled on the facts. Your inner eyes receive better illumination and understanding. You have started the process of rightful association. All your thoughts are now well focused, and you are discovering tomorrow with passion. You can easily see where you are going to. Your relationship with God is improving, because with Him all things are possible. He is giving you wisdom now and your thoughts are becoming established (Proverbs 16:3).

- You become more captivated with what you have discovered so far. Your vision is clearly spelt out in your heart. The name and the logo is in place. You are becoming more quiet and sensitive, as you begin to put the knowledge gained to work. You withdraw more from those who you see would add no value to your dreams and aspirations. You are regurgitating the knowledge in your head more often at this moment and your thoughts are filled with the desire to see your vision live up to expectation. Your selective lifestyle may not go well with many people – especially those of your household. Gideon was reported to his own father after he had destroyed their family god Baal, but the father thought Baal should defend himself (Judges 6:31). In some other cases it may not be as easy as it was for Gideon's father to give that report. Your vision is receiving threats from those on whose behalf you are developing it in order to help them out of slavery, and those who hold them bound to slavery as it happened to Moses. Nevertheless, your heart beats for success.

- At this stage, you sing the vision. It is filled with the lights of success. And the purpose the vision will achieve is now a slogan in your heart.

It is time to rewind and play your vision like a movie before you, so as to see it surviving the stormy waters of decision taking. Take the first step towards the actualization of the vision. Tell the right audience. Watch out for vision crashers. The beginning might be rough, but the fulfilment of the purpose justifies the vision. Walk out your vision – if you don't do it, no one will do it for you.

CHAPTER FIFTEEN

LEADERSHIP SAFETY

If you value the safety of your vision, you mind who you reveal it to. This is why God had to give Aaron to Moses, and Moses only went back to Egypt after the King that hunted his life was dead. Jesus was only returned to the land of Israel after Herod had died.

I would want us to look at the heart of Moses as he took his cherished people into the wilderness. What was going on in his mind? The only hope he had was God's conversation with him over the few months he had come to know him. He also relied on the experience he had after he escaped the land of Egypt for safety, so he was sure that the people would be safe as long as they would listen to him. The big question there is; how will he make them listen to him and act as he says? Jesus reaffirmed this over and over to the disciples that the only way they would be safe was if they would hearken unto His voice. God even spoke from heaven that everyone needs to hear Jesus so as to enjoy freedom.

Now as a man who runs his home, which automatically makes him a leader, he would yet see that while he has provided the doors in the house, they are often left unlocked at night. I have seen this happen to me several times. The beauty of safety is that it is everyone's responsibility, but it is more of a leader's responsibility who has to provide the framework upon which the safety of all will depend.

Going by what we have said above, we see that safety is about securing oneself and others from danger, harm or evil. Defence and safety are alike, but safety must take place to reduce active defence. Let us take a look at what the parents of Jesus would have done if they hadn't taken Him down to Egypt for safety as ordered by God – maybe they would have hired the services of security agents, if there had been any at that time, to defend the family against the hired murderers of Herod. But with divine instruction they were secured from the plot of danger that would have befallen them. If the people are safe they will appreciate the defence strategy we are putting in place. In the church, a pastor who is always intimidating his congregation with spiritual warfare prayers often renders powerless the faith in the members, and they start living in fear. Jesus told the Pharisees that as long as He was there, the disciples need not to bother so much about the much publicised fasting and prayer, which yielded no result. We must feel secure and safe before we can help others out of spiritual prison houses.

'People lack knowledge and their glory has been turned into shame' – Hosea 4:6-7. This implies that a leader who feeds those he leads with knowledge is securing them from the dangers that would befall them. Several times in the Bible, the voice of the Lord would come to His prophets to warn the Israelites about the evil that would befall them if they failed to repent. This is what I see as safety.

Safety is the act of taking proactive precautions against failure. To this end we would take a look at what I would call the aspects of leadership safety:

1. **Information safety:** This is very important to your success as a leader, because your attackers work with the information they have about you to bring your vision down. In your home, know those who come visiting. They may be the ones these attackers will use later to strangle life out your vision. If you are a male leader, mind how you come close to ladies. If you are a female leader, mind how you are seen with men. Wagging tongues don't ask questions before they publish you in the news. The other side of information safety has to do with leaders listening to lies. The Bible says in Proverbs 29:12: 'If a ruler hearken to lies, all his servants are wicked'. Imagine a leader with wicked followers, what will become of his vision? I would advise that every leader should mind what they listen to and know the integrity of who brings information to them, else they will soon lose grip of the vision they are driving.

2. **Emotional safety:** The Bible says in Proverbs 19:19: 'A man of great wrath shall suffer punishment: for if thou deliver him, yet thou must do it again'. Many leaders who end up as drug addicts often get into that trap as a result of emotional imbalance. As a leader, your emotional safety is of paramount interest to those you lead. We are also told: 'He shall not cry, nor lift up, nor cause his voice to be heard in the street' – Isaiah 42:1. The survival of your marriage often depends on how emotionally safe you are. Leaders are often sympathetic to the feelings of the opposite sex, which may become a trap to set them up. Emotional safety has a lot to do with emotional focus. Christ says your heart will be where your treasure is. A leader sees every other thing as secondary. If this is the case with your style of leadership, then be sure to set the boundaries on how your emotions operate. If you focus on the vision you are driving and see how anyone coming in contact with you can help the vision to succeed, then you will experience leadership emotional safety.

3. **Integrity safety:** As a leader people watch all you do and often judge you with an integrity yardstick. It is said of Jesus in Isaiah 42:3: 'A bruised reed shall he not break, and the smoking flax shall he not quench: he shall bring forth judgment unto truth'. And throughout His earthly life, He showed forth this principle of integrity safety.

How can a leader know that his integrity safety is on course at all times? He does an integrity reality check on his vision statement and operational mission statements to know if he is still within the path he earlier defined and explained to those he leads. He also conducts an integrity audit on those working for him. He confirms in his spirit that no evil thought is in his heart or unearned money has found its way into his bank account, and that he hasn't been dating a lady outside his marriage, etc. Our conscience is the best integrity reliability monitor God has given to each and every one of us. As a leader you should ask yourself if your integrity is intact. Many leaders, in trying to keep to their word, have murdered innocent people. One such instance was when Herod beheaded John the Baptist to please his wife, whose desire was disguise in his daughter's request, because John the Baptist had accused Herod of breaking the law for marrying his brother's wife. Another instance would be seen in Jephthah's decision to sacrifice his only daughter and only child in fulfilment of the vow he made before the Lord in Judges 11:30-40. In the two instances above, both leaders knew that it was morally wrong and not acceptable before God, but they did it to put their integrity in check. This is to show us the extent of how a leader will assess his integrity. In the examples above, I believe these leaders would have seek the face of God before going ahead with their actions and I am sure the Lord would have provided a solution.

4. Spiritual safety: I am concerned about how people visit all manner of spiritualists in order to secure their leadership positions, even in the church. What makes a leader spiritually safe is his relationship with God. The Bible says in 1 Corinthians 2:15-16: 'But he that is spiritual judgeth all things, yet he himself is judged of no man. For who hath known the mind of the Lord, that he may instruct him? but we have the mind of Christ.' Having the mind of Christ is what brings about spiritual safety. This is why every leader must be ready to lead the people in such a way that they will have fear for God, so that leaders will not start having people grumbling for lack of satisfaction as they work with them.

5. Financial safety: Many visions have died because of lack of financial safety. There was no limit to borrowing. In most cases, the investment they had became collaterals. This is not how to do business. Some churches even go to the extent of using church properties in taking loans which they now struggle to pay, and the whole essence of preaching about sanctity in the house of God is washed down to 'fund raising at all cost.' There and then, the church will lose its spiritual sense of being. A good plan will deliver any organisation from financial jeopardy. Every leader, from the home front, should be able to manage wasteful expenses by setting boundaries on what money should be spent on through resource planning.

6. **Cultural safety:** Every organisation lives in a culture. This is why new employees are indoctrinated so that they will get used to the acculturation practice inherent in the organisation. A leader should ask how he is fairing with the culture of the vision he is driving. Cultural safety has a way of affecting all we have been discussing, because it has to do with the mind. The culture in an organisation is a commonplace way of life within the organisation, and failure to adapt would mean your views are going to become unpopular. This is mostly related to a hired leader who has not been part of the vision maturation process. This is the same reason most organisations prefer to grow their leaders.

Safety, as I said in the beginning, has to do with securing those you lead from danger, harm or evil. To practice leadership safety, you must live it yourself. Only then will those you lead imbibe the culture of safety in all the spheres of leadership exercise of duty explained above.

CHAPTER SIXTEEN

LEADERSHIP DISCIPLESHIP

We need more leaders who have the discipleship characteristic inborn in them. Often what we see are those who claim to be leaders yet find it difficult to be submissive. Leadership discipleship is a phenomenon I want to use to explain the character of submissiveness in leaders. We have dealt with submission earlier on as it relates to our due diligence to the will of God. Here we will discuss how leaders would serve those they lead better. This is when leaders become servants and followers of the vision they drive.

A quick understanding of what we would be discussing could be gotten from Isaiah 9:6, where we are told that the government will be upon the shoulder of Jesus, referring to the burden of our sins which He would bear at His death.

We all know that it is only servants that take the dirt out of the home. Sins are like dirt, and since Jesus bore our sins, He qualified as one who had a servant heart. He also showed this at the washing of the feet event in John 13:5-15. To tell us that it was never a practice for a leader to wash disciples' feet, see how Peter reacted: 'Peter saith unto him, Thou shalt never wash my feet'. The only way a leader would have a discipleship spirit is when that leader is humble. Jesus submitted unto John the Baptist to be baptised of him. To also show that it was not supposed to be the order, let us see how John reacted to Jesus' request to be baptised by John – Matthew 3:14: 'But John forbad him, saying, I have need to be baptized of thee, and comest thou to me?' This is leadership discipleship in action.

The act of leadership provision is an act of service. What we see mostly today are leaders who only care about their selfish desires, leaving the larger populace in penury. Even in the church, we have the poor being decimated daily by these greedy leaders. Leadership discipleship is the beauty of submissiveness. Breakaways in churches, for instance, are the result of lack of the spirit of submission, and we also find that such leaders don't take instruction from God.

The reason why many leaders lack the discipleship attribute of service is often tied to their expectation and the immediate gains they want to get. We see this in the political world, especially in the developing world, where leaders scuttle the wealth of the states they are supposed to serve and store it in foreign bank accounts. Disloyalty in leaders is because they don't have the discipleship quality in them. A leader who has a discipleship spirit will always put himself in his followers' shoes and see from that angle what they may be in need of. That way, he would adjust himself to communicate effectively to others to ensure they are equipped to function productively in his team.

Jesus was so sure of the kind of training He had given to His disciples that He could boast that they would do more exploits than they saw Him perform. This was because He saw it from their own perspective, having known the training curriculum and empowerment they had undergone. We have other instances to demonstrate the fact that Jesus was actually one with a servant heart:

- He bore His own cross, until He was assisted (Luke 23:26). Even today, many leaders would want someone who would bear their bags as a show of respect to their authority, and when this is not done they would make remarks about it.

- He was the same as His disciples. This was why Judas had to betray Him with a kiss. When they came to arrest Him, He offered Himself that He was the one they were looking for, otherwise they would not have known (John 18:4-8). There are many leaders who would want that distinction to show to the extent that when one comes into their operating vicinity, their bossy nature will show they are in charge. People have come to our church telling me they want to see the pastor, and I tell them to sit down. It is only when they are later led to me that they realise it was me they were looking for.

- When John the Baptist revealed Jesus to his disciples they followed Him, showing us that He was indeed like every other person who walked by daily – John 1:36-37.

In the continuing discussion below, we discuss what leaders need to do to imbibe the leadership discipleship spirit:

1. A leader should see his reward above this physical world: 'who for the joy that was set before him endured the cross, despising the shame, and is set down at the right hand of the throne of God.' - Hebrews 12:2.

2. A leader must know that his approval by God is tied to his good works in the lives of those he leads: 'Let your light so shine before men, that they may see your good works, and glorify your Father which is in heaven.' - Matthew 5:16.

3. A leader should know that in order to live a legacy that will stand the test of time, he needs to replicate his ideas in the hearts of those he leads, implying that he has to come to their understanding sometimes. Jesus did this while he was teaching in parables to the teeming crowd and in pure language to his disciples. Jesus taught us that He did not come to break the law but to fulfil it (Matthew

5:17). Your disciples should live the vision you preached after you are dead. We have scientific inventions that are still relevant today, hundreds of years after they were invented. See the vision you are driving as an invention that should live on after your death.

4. Adequate remuneration for those who work with a leader is only possible when a leader puts himself in the shoes of those he leads, knowing that they will eventually visit the same market he visits to purchase the same things he would want.

5. A leader who has the discipleship spirit in him will show appreciation to those he leads always – verbally and materially. A get-together dinner will do even more than expected. This is a motivation boost that will make them becoming resilient as they help you to drive the vision you bear.

6. A leader who prays for those he leads is one with a discipleship spirit. This act of his will make those he leads respond with a loyalty spirit.

CHAPTER SEVENTEEN

LEADERSHIP SELF-DISCOVERY

The process of self-discovery is continuous. This is why leaders attend conferences and leadership workshops to learn from others' experiences and share their own. As we mingle with people daily, we often become better in our leadership drive, since we shed most of the dry, unproductive leaves in our lives and prune off the branches that have become unproductive. This helps us to plan effectively and make maximum use of the resources at our disposal.

Every leader must know his/her strengths and weaknesses. Isaiah 30:15 talked of the renewing of strength. Those he referred to certainly did not know that they needed to renew their strength, because they were not aware that they had become unproductive. We must discover our potentials and gifts, and also know our failures. People don't want to be told when they go wrong. Jabez prayed for an enlarged territory and against causing pain to others, because he knew the meaning of his name, and we were told that his request was granted: 'he was more honourable than his brothers. His mother had named him Jabez, saying, 'I gave birth to him in pain.' Jabez cried out to the God of Israel, saying, 'Oh that you would bless me and enlarge my territory! Let your hand be with me, and keep me from harm so that I will be free from pain.' And God granted his request.' – 1 Chronicles 4:9-10(NIV).

A leader should see ahead of him in order to know what may befall him in the near future as a result of inabilities in his cadre of leadership. The sources of the predicaments we might face in the years ahead sometimes look very passive, and could be hidden just as Jabez' predicament was hidden in his name. Let us see how Jabez intercepted what would have befallen him through self-discovery:

- He knew the meaning of his name. We have also seen that God changed names often in the Bible to establish a purpose in the lives of those he used as leaders. Every leader should know what their names stand for. The next thing every leader would do is to also understand the meaning of the name of the vision they are driving. If it is a company, the name should represent increase and not pain. This is how a leader should think. Even the not-too-obvious problems need your attention as a leader. Sometimes the leader may decide to look the other way on issues that may not be of importance, but then he needs to have a thorough overview of all the issues before him.

- Jabez cried to the God of Israel because he was aware that He answered prayers. It is not about discovering the faults in our lives, it is how we seek for solution to turn the seemingly ugly situation around us to good that helps us establish the purpose of the vision we drive as leaders. At every progress review opportunity, leaders should see that they seek help from God in prayers and anyone they know would have a solution to the leadership ills they are facing.

- As leaders we should know that when we experience pains in our leadership drive we shouldn't forget to see the brighter side of life. Jabez prayed for blessings from God – and that God should enlarge his territory.

Tools needed for leadership self-discovery:

- Progress review meetings: This is where operational policies, ideas, plans, etc, are checked against the success of the vision you are driving. A time came (Isaiah 1:18) when God called on His children to gather for a progress review. Even in Psalms 50:5 God asked that those who believe in Him through their sacrificial act to be gathered unto Him. During a progress review, what you do as a leader is more of a winnowing effort aimed at reducing wastage. An effective progress review meeting will provide answers to the problems the vision is facing. During your review you will know how far or near you are to achieving the goals of the vision.

- Leadership assessment: There are established organisations that do leadership assessments. In some organisations, those you lead may be given questionnaires to assess your personality and leadership initiatives. The reports are fed back to you as a leader for you to know the areas for self improvement. This is because the success of your vision lies with your perceptions – physical and spiritual.

- Subordinates' performance: The performance of your subordinates as leaders is sometimes related to how you lead. This means you could use their performance reports to assess how you are faring in your leadership drive.

- Seeking the face of God: Praying, fasting and meditation have the power to create both spiritual and physical awakening in us. Such awakening can usually make you more focused on the vision you are driving.

- Studying the Bible: With its plethora of wisdom, the Bible is a sure resource bank. No leader will succeed without studying the Bible daily, especially the books of Proverbs, Ecclesiastes and Psalms.

- Reading related books: We have millions of books that have been written all over the world. People write from their experiences, and through their own experience you can develop yourself with the advice given to become more effective, knowing that someone else has passed through the rough waters you are experiencing. I have developed over the years through the books I have read.

- Attending seminars and workshops: this creates the avenue for creativity training. We interact with other leaders through this avenue and lessons learned are shared across borders.

- Counselling others will help you learn: I learned from those I counsel daily, as they have lots of experiences to share.

- Group work/team-building events: As a leader, you should encourage team culture. Teamwork helps a leader to share experiences across teams. This is most effective during team-building events. The challenges affecting the vision are tabled and discussed, while the way forward is also discussed in an open-minded way without those you lead being afraid of victimization and losing their job.

- Media power: There is what is called 'agenda setting' in mass media broadcasting. The media have the power to change the way people think. Seeing movies and documentaries/histories, listening to news and recorded teachings, reading news magazines, browsing the internet, etc, have a way of developing a leader.

- Vision reality inquiry: We need to gather information about how far we are striving within the dictate of the vision, sometime comparing our exploits with those of leaders championing similar visions.

CHAPTER EIGHTEEN

LEADERSHIP ACCEPTABILITY

A leader who forces himself on the people or those he intends to lead is a dictator. Leadership acceptance in principle and fact is a two-edged sword: one edge faces God while the other faces the people he leads. The following are the various instances of leadership acceptability:

• **Accepted by the people, rejected by God:**

This is the fate of all fake prophets. The people who run after signs and wonders easily accept these sets of money making prophets, unaware that they are rejected by God. King Saul also faced this kind of acceptance. The people still saw him as their king; meanwhile, God had already anointed David. The same goes with Eli, though the people complained of the atrocities of his sons, but he was not ousted out of office - his presence in that office was not welcomed by God any longer until God raised Samuel in his stead. Many political leaders who rule as governors, presidents, etc, are also not in good standing with God, hence the people they lead are grumbling under the weight of deprivation.

• Accepted by God, rejected by the people:

We have a clear example of this when the Bible says that Jesus went into His own and His own rejected Him. John 1:10-12: 'He was in the world, and the world was made by Him, and the world knew him not. He came unto his own, and his own received him not. But as many as received him, to them gave he power to become the sons of God, even to them that believe on his name...' This was why He was unable to achieve much in His own home town. This is mainly the fate of God-raised leaders. The people reject them because they carry with them a whip of righteousness aimed at correcting the evil in society.

The Bible says in John 3:19-20: 'And this is the condemnation, that light is come into the world, and men loved darkness rather than light, because their deeds were evil. For every one that doeth evil hateth the light, neither cometh to the light, lest his deeds should be reproved'. The multitudes of evil in society are caused by evil people and they are readily seen within the corridors of power, which they hold on to, so as to remain relevant in the eyes of the people. But it is easy for the oppressed to know a God-chosen leader as he can vouch for the presence of God in whatever he does.

• Rejected by God, rejected by the people:

This has happened in many nations of the world. These leaders are dictators and have no fear of God. Those they lead are hungry in the midst of plenty, and their acts makes God visit the nation with pestilence and untold calamities. Those they claim to lead have no attachment to their ideals and vision, but they force themselves to be accepted. When they visit the populace for campaigns, political leaders pay the people to attend and to transport them to the arena where the meeting will be held. They rely mostly on the media for selfish egotistic propaganda.

This may happen even in the church. Many claiming to have been called by God are only there to satisfy their wants, because they see the church as a means of employment when all attempts to get a well-paid job outside have failed. In these churches, their messages are corrupted by continuous demands for offerings and fund-raising appeals, while neglecting the main purpose of the calling, which is to preach repentance and the renewal of the mind.

God is moved when we genuinely repent. Here is what God says concerning the King of Judah who repented and tore his clothes (2 Chronicles 34:14-19), on hearing the words of the Laws of Moses: 'Because thine heart was tender, and thou didst humble thyself before God, when thou heardest his words against this place, and against the inhabitants thereof, and humbledst thyself before me, and didst rend thy clothes, and weep before me; I have even heard thee also, saith the Lord. Behold, I will gather thee to thy fathers, and thou shalt be gathered to thy grave in peace, neither shall thine eyes see all the evil that I will bring upon this place, and upon the inhabitants of the same...' - 2 Chronicles 34:27-28.

If a leader can make peace with God, he will make peace with the people he leads.

• Accepted by God, accepted by the people:

This is the platform upon which peace and tranquillity will thrive. A verse of the Bible that defines this platform of leadership acceptability is Proverbs 29:2: 'When the righteous are in authority, the people rejoice: but when the wicked beareth rule, the people mourn'. Although this is a rare occurrence, which soon degenerates into any of the three above. A week before Jesus' crucifixion, He was accepted by the people with a hosanna song. But these same people accused him of insolent behaviour and made up their mind to do away with Him. To tell us the gravity of their decision, see what Jesus said in Luke 23:28-30: 'But Jesus turning unto them said, Daughters of Jerusalem, weep not for me, but weep for yourselves, and for your children. For, behold, the days are coming, in the which they shall say, Blessed are the barren, and the wombs that never bare, and the paps which never gave suck. Then shall they begin to say to the mountains, Fall on us; and to the hills, Cover us'.

We would see instances of this platform of acceptability in the Bible – King Saul, King David, King Solomon, etc. The Bible commended King David in 2 Samuel 8:15: 'And David reigned over all Israel; and David executed judgment and justice unto all his people'. Though David was widely accepted, his own son wanted him dead.

The Doctrine of Acceptability opined that for one to lead successfully, he/she must be accepted by the people and also accepted by God. This is what is termed 'vox populi'. Psalms 24:3-4 defines what is expected of a leader who will be accepted by God: 'Who shall ascend into the hill of the Lord? or who shall stand in his holy place? He that hath clean hands, and a pure heart; who hath not lifted up his soul unto vanity, nor sworn deceitfully'.

The following are the attributes of a leader who is accepted by both God and the people:

- Peace and tranquillity is one of the obvious signs that God is with a leader. When a leader assumes a leadership position and all of a sudden, there is chaos, just like the plagues of Egypt is a clear indication that God is not with him.

- Generosity and hospitality spring into existence in the hearts of the people. When the people live in hatred, want and fear, then the head has a problem. Jesus always calmed the storm.

- Obedience is also seen among the people. The young ones obey their elders. Children obey their parents, and then the entire people, including the leader, obey God.

- Leadership ideas and instructions are followed to the letter, because such a leader works and walk in righteousness. Proverbs 24:26 says: 'Every man shall kiss his lips that giveth a right answer'. Those he leads see his opinion as the right answer to their predicaments.

CHAPTER NINETEEN

LEADERSHIP EXCELLENCE

Excellence is a measure of the level of acceptance the leader is receiving. A rejected leader can never perform, because effective leadership can only thrive in a peaceful environment where there is a cordial relationship between the leader and those he leads.

I want to start this chapter with this verse of the Bible: 'I have taught thee in the way of wisdom; I have led thee in right paths' - Proverbs 4:11. Now let's see other instances of what God said to His new-found leaders. To Gideon, God said, 'Have not I sent you?' (Judges 6:14) To Joshua He said, 'Have I not commanded you?' (Joshua 1:9) I want us to ponder over these statements from God to these leaders. In the proverb referred to above, God is talking to us. The tone of the verse simply explains what could seem like giving a final instruction to a child before he/she begins a long journey, where he/she may scarcely consult his/her mentor, maybe due to the task of the new responsibility before him/her.

Now let's see this: 'The excellence of knowledge is that wisdom gives life to them that have it' - Ecclesiastes 7:12. To them that have what? - That have wisdom of course. To lead with excellence is only possible through divine wisdom. Without wisdom, no leader would be able to take a successful decision, as explained in Proverbs 8:2: 'She standeth in the top of high places, by the way in the places of the paths'. The last statement there talks of the paths – this is the point of decision making. This is why leadership is all about growth and development in wisdom, knowledge and understanding. This is also why proud people fail in leadership. In Job 37:23, Job confessed that indeed God is excellent in power and in judgement, and plenty of justice. What does these attributes of the leadership quality of God tell us? They tell us simply that those whom God orders their footsteps, who hence become righteous, are going to lead excellently.

The Lord says in Proverbs 4:11-13: 'I have taught thee in the way of wisdom; I have led thee in right paths. When thou goest, thy steps shall not be straitened; and when thou runnest, thou shalt not stumble. Take fast hold of instruction; let her not go: keep her; for she is thy life'. And this opens up a concern for today's leaders – to teach wisdom and lead others in right paths, so that excellence will thrive.

God is saying that He can only lead us in the right paths (Isaiah 42:16). This is where leadership excellence comes from. Joshua and Gideon were both excellent leaders because they submitted to the ultimate leadership guidance of God. The Bible says that Daniel was ten times better than his counterparts (Daniel 1:20). This is excellence in display. Servicing is providing support and offering oneself selflessly to see that others come into the limelight. It involves taking people through the path of growth, where they pick up the lessons of life, which they will use as background knowledge to solve problems that will add value to others.

Now knowledge is resident on the facts of life experiences which we have in our hands. When we are able to apply knowledge resourcefully, we end up being seen as one with the spirit of excellence. Serving, either in the government or public organisations, without the resourceful application of knowledge, is an act of foolishness. Unwise judgements are seen as foolish acts. We can also say that foolishness in our hearts is what clouds the wisdom of God, which we should have applied to solve problems. King Solomon was wise, and as long as he applied wisdom, he ruled excellently. But the moment he derailed, he fell from grace to shame.

Leadership excellence leads to the following:

- A solution providing leadership is always in place in both proactive and reactive situations.

- Superior decision making process in place, with all the

facts clearly spelt out. No mistakes. All actions are well articulated, planned and carried out, with the right resources.

- The act of mediocrity is not popular among those you lead. Wisdom is seen in all they do.

- Leadership achievements spell distinction all the time and are easily distinguished from other organisations with similar visions.

- A successor is readily available to carry on in the event of the death of the present leader.

Leadership excellence is a culture that grows with your vision as you make mistakes and learn from them. It involves lots of documentation works, so that as time goes on the leadership operational ethical standard is established, followed and monitored to see that it works. This is what gives birth to excellence. In Biblical terms, excellence is seen as perfection or holiness. This is why those in political seats of power often want to be addressed as 'his/her Excellency.' The Bible in Haggai 2:12 gives a picture of what could hinder leadership excellence by inference: 'if someone carries consecrated meat in the fold of their garment, and that fold touches some bread or stew, some wine, olive oil or other food, does it become consecrated?' The priests answered, 'No." The mere fact that one is called a leader does not make him one who will deliver on promise unless such a leader has yielded to our Holy God, which now makes the leader righteous.

This is what we can infer from the verse above. Serving under a consecrated servant of God does not make one consecrated because one has to undergo the process of concentration as approved by God. In the same way, a leader would act excellently, doing things exceptionally when such a leader undergoes a development process, which increases his wealth of experience, and his willingness to learn, adopt and adapt to best practices that would lead to leadership excellence.

Leadership excellence is borne out of maturity in knowledge and understanding. I want to make an inference from Isaiah 11:6: 'The wolf also shall dwell with the lamb, and the leopard shall lie down with the kid; and the calf and the young lion and the fatling together; and a little child shall lead them'. A little child is leading with excellence because the devourers have become friendly with the devoured – they have decided to live in peace because the knowledge of Christ has filled the earth. This is why any leader who imposes himself on the people he leads will not see his leadership thrive. The people must have agreed to live together as one family before the leadership can take root. The man would see himself as a leader, the woman would see herself as a leader and the children would see themselves as leaders of tomorrow only when they all understand the purpose of their existence in the society where they live. Then leadership will take root in everyone's consciousness. There is no way we can have leadership excellence when there is anarchy.

Joseph's excellence in dream interpretation took him from want to affluence. A time came after his death when a pharaoh who knew him not came into power and his people became slaves, pointing to the fact that no matter what you have achieved as a leader, the moment there is a change in government your works may no longer receive popularity. What baffles me is that despite the stories that shows how Joseph helped Egypt, why would anybody of the order and calibre of a king such as Pharaoh not recognise Joseph and thereafter treat his people with regard?

How do we then explain leadership excellence in the face of this negligence of posterity by the ruling class in many quarters? The fear of this is the reason why many who have the opportunity to lead often see that position as their last opportunity to make wealth and enrich their families. Joseph would have sent his family back to Canaan after the famine instead of leaving them in the land of Goshen, were it some of our leaders today. Imagine someone like Joseph, who had so much authority, yet his people were treated with disdain and hilarious disregard. Leadership excellence thrives where there is selfless service.

CHAPTER TWENTY

DYNAMIC LEADERSHIP

A dynamic leader thinks of excellence. Those you lead want to feel the pulse of a leader. They want to hear his breath and footsteps behind to give them the assurance of direction and safety.

I once sampled an opinion from people over a question that was in my heart: if you are to travel on foot with your wife and the instruction says that you must not look behind you or speak as you walk, which of you will take the lead so that the other will follow?

The responses were varied. The men wanted their wives to take the lead for the purpose of providing safety for her so that she would be confident to take the walk. While some ladies agreed to this, others were sceptical, saying the man might decide to turn back after a while, leaving them alone to walk on. The ladies also asked how they would know if the man became tired and needed rest. These ladies preferred to be at the back, and then they also realised that if they become tired, the man ahead will not know, especially knowing that their footsteps may not sound as loud and hard as those of men. What is your opinion? This is the fact a leader deals with daily. He assumes the position of one leading and at the same time the position of one behind.

When I heard of the death of the Al Qaeda leader Osama Bin Laden in the early hours of the 2nd of May 2011, something came to my mind. What was the vision he had died for? A dynamic leader dies for visions that bring succour and peace to those he/she leads. In a changing society, the dynamic leader ensures that those they lead are not engulfed in helpless situations, as Jesus did when He begged those who came to arrest Him to let His disciples go unhurt. After his death, what would happen to those he was leading? First they would ever remain in hiding, and would be seen as public enemies by those who hunted them throughout these years. The families of the those who died in the World Trade Centre on September 11 2001 might never forgive him, even at death.

We should be able to ask ourselves these questions. Are we causing the populace pain as a result of our actions? Can we judge that the actions we carry out are well thought through? A dynamic leader bears the pains of those He leads, just as the government is upon Jesus' shoulder.

Another instance I want to recall to mind is the militancy era in Nigeria, which lasted from 2006 to 2010. These groups claimed that they were fighting a genuine cause, and their leaders recruited more hands to help them fight the guerrilla war in the creeks of the Niger Delta.

Soon those they were fighting for, the poor inhabitants of the dirty and oil-polluted creeks of the Delta, who had to continuously looked to God for a sip of good water only when it rained, started complaining and shouting for help. Innocent women and young girls were being raped by these now-animalized persons. It became a hunt, and the untamed politician used them to meet ends. People rushed to God to pray for this to end.

Some of the government security forces who should have helped the situation connived with these militias and started the exploitation of crude oil pipes and the scavenging of the fuel-ready condensate, which they now marketed to the public. Many lives were lost when this fake fuel went into the kerosene stoves of the same poor people, whom they had eagerly convinced the world that they were representing. Kidnapping was on the increase, children became victims and the government paid lip service to the safety of the oppressed people, in this propagandisation of a militarised hellhole. The situation was chaotic. The 'loose ends' in society, popularly called armed bandits, took to the streets with handguns to make life even more unbearable. It was as if crime was legalised, from Delta State to Cross Rivers State - the story was the same everywhere in the oil-rich Delta. And it went into the towns of Aba, and started moving up North.

This was a locust-spreading inferno, and the pains went even deeper in the hearts of Nigerians. Those who started the fight were already losing ground too as those whom they recruited no longer obeyed them, and often broke out to start a camp of their own. There and then they realised that they had lost focus of the objective of their fight. Guns and ammunitions were in the streets. Education was decaying, and who cared? After all, there were graduates roaming the streets as hopeless, helpless and disease-prone vagrants.

This situation above was due to the failure of dynamic leadership. It called for a demonstration of leadership which was never there. Those they were there to protect took to the streets to condemn their actions, because people were dying in anguish. And the government in the centre thought it wise to provide amnesty to anyone who wanted it; this was accepted by the big names in the fight after much consideration and plea from the political class, who obviously felt they could be used to upturn election results, since elections were around the corner. This was just the way the Israelites felt they could use Jephthah, who was already living as an outlaw to help them defeat the Ammonites, in Judges 11:3-6: 'Then Jephthah fled from his brethren, and dwelt in the land of Tob: and there were gathered vain men to

Jephthah, and went out with him. And it came to pass in process of time, that the children of Ammon made war against Israel. And it was so, that when the children of Ammon made war against Israel, the elders of Gilead went to fetch Jephthah out of the land of Tob: And they said unto Jephthah, Come, and be our captain, that we may fight with the children of Ammon'. We could liken the process of the call to Jephthah by the same people who drove him out as an amnesty call.

The Nigerian amnesty call motives were varied, for whoever cared to know and seek the so-called amnesty. The church prayed for it, others prayed they should be brought to book, and some others felt God could forgive them if they were bold enough to accept Christ. I belong to the last group anyway.

The amnesty by the government was a step in the direction of dynamic leadership. This is because it ended the then politico-guerrilla war conflagration and further destruction that would have resulted, which was almost leading to the desolation of the major cities in the Niger Delta region. The city of Warri was getting more and more desolate by the day as more people and companies moved out.

Before this time the ruling political class had thought it wise to give a political seat to a native of the land to quell the militia powers that were rising. This decision brought in a son of the land into the seat of the Vice President, and as if God was at work, he also became the president. They shifted ground to find a solution to the ailing situation at least, and the other argument was, 'will it ever work?' Of course it never worked, as the calmness is now gradually returning back to a state of anarchy. This also is failure in dynamic leadership. A dynamic leader educates the minds of those he leads so that they will not appreciate evil.

From the examples I just gave we can define dynamic leadership as positive leadership in a chaotic situation. Positive leadership steers the ship to shore after surviving a heavy storm at sea.

A leader is seen to be dynamic when the following happens:

- Chaotic situations are foreseen ahead of time and they are calmed before they degenerate into situations that would cause irreparable losses.

- When they do occur, the dynamic leader will show leadership presence throughout the period to ensure normality is returned.

- At the end of the turmoil, the dynamic leader takes those he leads through a training process to educate them further, and adequate punishment is meted out on those who erred to deter others from carrying out such acts.

- He sees himself as the solution to every situation.

- He works with well-laid plans and processes, if they exist, otherwise he devises a process that has worked elsewhere and yielded results.

- He can in some cases take decisions that defy well-known processes.

- He is a leader of leaders. He checks that his leadership thrives with joy in the heart in those he leads.

- Though a dynamic leader is not necessarily a stick of dynamite set to explode, he surely knows when to cut off the strings. This is how he applies his leadership authority over critical issues in some cases.

CHAPTER TWENTY ONE

THE MAKING OF A LEADER

Some say leaders are born; others say leadership qualities can be developed in an individual. Which school of thought do you belong to? The fable of 'who shall bell the cat' reminds us how difficult it is to have a leader who is ready to face the obstacles of leadership, break through them and lead others across.

I still remember growing up in my home. My mother was barren for eight years before finally I was born. This would have automatically made me the leader in the house. Then I noticed that while my parents disciplined me whenever I erred, and the lessons had been passed into me, I would want to discipline my younger ones as if trying to make them go through what I was going through in the hands of my parents, only to see my parents coming against me and defending them. I saw it as hatred, feeling that my parents indeed hated me. My relationship with everybody in my home grew cold by the day, as I started withdrawing from everyone to avoid being beaten with the whip. I was finding joy outside, and then I also encountered hatred from those who I thought were going to accept me because of my brilliant academic performance.

One day I was beaten up by a group of boys for topping the class in the primary school. I became more afraid of driving for excellence as hatred multiplied by the day. While in many African homes the eldest child is seen as a leader, his leadership is restricted to provision, as he/she has to train and provide for his/her younger ones once he is gainfully employed, or even before that. Some young ladies have confessed that as the eldest in their homes they decided to go into prostitution to help their families – this is leadership sacrifice. I am only relating these stories to activate your own perspective of how one becomes a leader.

Eventually I left home, seeking freedom and acceptance. I am the sort of person who is ready to go against the crowd to put things right, and my home and wherever I found myself were not ready for that kind of aggressive orderliness. This is how I knew that I was in the wrong circle. My desire then was to come out someday to confront these wrongs. I wrote my first manuscript, which was supposed to be a novel entitled *What a man does*. It became a tragedy that decried what evil men do in secret and told of their horrible end. Though, somehow I lost it, I am still searching for the manuscript.

Others followed and then there were poems, none published. But even then, the tones and the messages in them tell the story of me against the crowd and the accepted ugly norms in the society. Then gradually, my eyes went into the church and their doctrinal practices. I wasn't baptised then, but I was born again, in the sense that I now had a renewed heart, to confront evil – this is what I see as born again, not the doctrinal beliefs in many churches today.

Christ's spirit referred to in Galatians 4:6 is a spirit that confronts anomalies and evil practices and wields itself to correct them. Jesus lent credence to this fact when He said in Mark 9:38-40: 'And John answered him, saying, Master, we saw one casting out devils in thy name, and he followeth not us: and we forbad him, because he followeth not us. But Jesus said, Forbid him not: for there is no man which shall do a miracle in my name, that can lightly speak evil of me. For he that is not against us is on our part'. The disciples wanted doctrine, but Jesus preferred action.

Then, as I said earlier, because I was finding it difficult to be accepted with my school of thought, I became even colder, avoiding people and being alone. That was how I developed the power of deep thinking, as I tried to compare society practices with the Bible. When I became baptised in the St. Stephen Anglican church in Iluelogbo, now Owhelogbo in the Isoko-speaking area of Delta State in Nigeria, my quest for freedom increased. This act of mine continued. Even though I tried to mingle with people, I discovered that I couldn't cope with a lot of things – their habits, attitudes, and characters. I had tried to smoke, drink, womanize, etc but every time I would go back home crying and regretting my acts. I was wondering why those I mingled with weren't feeling the same way I did. I felt then that I might be abnormal after all, and I was hiding in my shame, since I thought what they were doing was the right thing to be accepted in society.

Then the calling came. From 2005 to 2008, my change was easily noticed. I had withdrawn from many people who had been my friends. I was getting more withdrawn from people and minding my own business, so to speak. Though I had been given a red Bible in one of my dreams in 1994, it didn't dawn on me that I was being sent an errand of deliverance by God through the word.

From that day in 1994 my wisdom had been increasing, and this was helping me to manage my life, apparently against the wish of my parents in most cases. So when the calling came, I was battling with the same acceptance, but this time from my heart as I felt nobody would believe I had been called by God because I hadn't gone to any of the Bible schools and could not quote scripture verses offhand. I fought this acceptance within my heart and I was getting drained up.

I had got married, in January 2004, and my wife had been

in the Catholic faith while I was in the Anglican faith. We mended our differences through Biblical beliefs and that created the avenue for us to confront wrong practices the more. We asked dozens of questions about what the church practised and our answers were popping up from the Bible, which gave us joy. The Holy Spirit of God was giving us more insight into the scriptures and a time came I started teaching the Bible.

Within this period, we also had a fellowship with Salvation Ministries in Port Harcourt Nigeria, where Pastor David Ibiyeomie officiates as the founding Pastor. Our understanding increased, and with the help of God our home became the Church's home cell centre for the Rumuodara axis, Port Harcourt. The church came into our home and learning how to officiate and minister was becoming more live in our hearts. My wife joined me in the study of the Bible more and more, and we became more withdrawn from the outside.

This was not going well with our parents. They no longer see us visiting as before. The wisdom of God was guiding us. We were becoming as wise as the serpent, withdrawing from public scrutiny and attacking so that we could mature our faith in Christ.

On the 19th of October 2008, the first public service of the church was celebrated with a total of 15 worshippers. Our neighbours joined us and we were happy to have a church in the neighbourhood. The message that came with the church wasn't a popular one. It was a message diffused with Jesus' concern in John 4:21-24. We also recorded the messages as I preached them unskilfully on Sundays. The messages were later transferred into text by my little sister-in-law Stephanie Ereme Jack, into what became my first book, *Existing in the Supernatural*. I commenced a school of ministry and about 15-20 persons were in attendance. My job didn't give me the time to continue with them, so it packed up – that was how I learned planning. Before this time, a young man started with me and later withdrew with the excuse that he wasn't called into a pulpit ministry, though he is now a pastor. While I was devastated, God strengthened me with a book I stumbled on – *The Mega Church* by Bishop Dag Heward Mills, Bishop of Lighthouse Chapel International in Ghana.

Later my wife began disagreeing with everything I was doing, as she felt she was losing my attention. Her attacking nature started sending many members running away, because they couldn't condone her quarrel with me. I was becoming a changed man. People quarrelled over my constantly switching off of my phones and not answering calls. They did not know what I was battling within me.

I was reading more books. I was discouraged from publishing my first book by some people who I thought would have supported me. I was getting withdrawn again as I struggled with acceptance. The second book had some editing issues and I was told I was in a hurry. I learned again. It was as if I was against all.

This book is the ninth I am writing after the release of my first book in November 2009. While it is difficult to tell how a leader is made, we find that God raises leaders because of the gifts He has put in them. These gifts help them to act in such a way that anyone who is around them will know such a person is the one who should take the lead naturally.

The maturity of any leader comes through his daily encounters with leadership challenges. This is why leadership is difficult to teach in organised classroom setting. It comes through the process of Encounter, Disagreement, Inquiry, Confrontation, Expectation, Learning, Instituting and Monitoring (EDICELIM). These will form the basis of what we would be discussing in this subject of how a leader comes to be.

• **Encounter process**

This has to do with how we interact with our environment daily. What we perceive with our senses and the interpretation thereof in our minds gradually start developing into both the acceptance and rejection of ideas, based on our inner instinct of what we perceive as right or wrong. This happened to Moses as he tried to save the Israelite who was being manhandled by the Egyptian. How did he come to this encounter for change?

It was because on a daily basis he was seeing how his people were suffering, as recorded in Exodus 2:11-12: 'Now it came to pass in those days, when Moses was grown, that he went out to his brethren and looked at their burdens. And he saw an Egyptian beating a Hebrew, one of his brethren. So he looked this way and that way, and when he saw no one, he killed the Egyptian and hid him in the sand.

• **Disagreement process**

The moment we are convinced that what is being practised is wrong, there is this inside disagreement within us. This is the beginning of the birth of a leader. The action of Moses in Exodus 2:12 shows that he disagreed with what he encountered. King Hezekiah even destroyed the bronze serpent that Moses made in the wilderness to save the children of Israel from the bite of snakes, because the children of Israel now sacrificed unto it and called it Nehushtan (2 Kings 18:4).

• **Inquiry process**

The leader to be inquires about what he has disagreed with in order to gain more knowledge and understanding. At this stage, he is voraciously searching through history. We would see this in Moses' capability to have written the book of Genesis, which contained events that happened before he was born. It is my thinking that Moses had commenced the writing of the book of Genesis long before he fled the house of Pharaoh into Midian. This I believe because of the several encounters of his ancestors with Egypt, and knowing that Egypt is a historical centre of world history, Moses may have gathered information about the origin of his people, which would have made him act as he did in Exodus 3:11-12.

• **Confrontation process**

Once he is assured of his stand, he confronts the status quo. This act will begin to raise followers for him, who believe in what he is fighting for but do not dare to face it. Such confrontation mostly includes the use of information dissemination. He takes his new followers through the knowledge that convinced him that the existing practices were wrong. They start coining a vision and mission statements. He preaches his beliefs wherever he goes, getting more hearers and believers. John the Baptist spoke of Jesus' capability to confront evil in Matthew 3:12: 'His winnowing fan is in His hand, and He will thoroughly clean out His threshing floor, and gather His wheat into the barn; but He will burn up the chaff with unquenchable fire.'

• **Expectation process**

He starts expecting reaction from the public – positive or negative. These reactions will strengthen him more to confront the questions that may have been raised. They prepare him for the task ahead as he now knows that he is creating an impact in the heart of the people, supportive or non-supportive of his intentions. This would be seen in Moses' expectation result in Exodus 2:13-14: And when he went out the second day, behold, two Hebrew men were fighting, and he said to the one who did the wrong, 'Why are you striking your companion?' Then he said, 'Who made you a prince and a judge over us? Do you intend to kill me as you killed the Egyptian?' So Moses feared and said, 'Surely this thing is known!' And that took him on the run for safety into a land, and an opportunity to learn and serve in the house of a Midian Priest. There, for the first time, Moses became a shepherd.

- **Learning process**

Here the growing leader learns from his mistakes, and as in the case of Moses, he starts learning shepherding and living under the same roof with his wife and in-laws; a show of humility, patience and tolerance. The leader may at this stage start developing strategies and training manuals to mature the hearts of those that will support and be ready to work and walk with him. The logo is live in his and in their hearts. The maturity process evolves for followers, which will qualify them to hold certain offices and undertake certain responsibilities.

- **Institution process**

This is the last phase of the making of a leader. Here he institutes all that will be. Further minor and major changes may be effected later on, but he has something to work with already, and the process just runs on auto. This is the beauty of the Ten Commandments of Moses, and we would also see it in the life of Jesus, who taught the principles of the Kingdom of God and the institution of the Holy Communion.

• Monitoring process

This is the leader in action, seeing that his vision is becoming a reality. He gathers more support of like minds. He encourages them to seek public offices in order to get across to the government and sell his ideas and reform policies. He makes use of the media more often, gaining support. All a leader does at this stage is gathering support and announcements so as to become a household name in the hearts of all and sundry.

Below are some quick pieces of advice that will help you as you strive in your leadership pursuit:

1. Selecting your workforce

Some people are naturally desperate in all things. They want to know their reward before they will work with you. At every time they want to know which authority you are relinquishing to them. They want to be seen everywhere and would want to be introduced alongside you when you are invited to a function. They are not ready to take your instructions – at every opportunity they have, they would want to grumble for others to hear in order to disapprove your leadership influence on them.

They are also very difficult to train. They have all the answers at their fingertips, even when they may be wrong. They hate corrections, especially when they come from the leader. Such persons will mar your leadership vision. Ensure that you select a workforce who will be loyal to you. This way you will be able to get your vision through. The non-desperate people may not be ready to work, but you need to encourage and train them to get them functioning.

- Coping with a desperate workforce: You must keep them busy at all times and be ready to force the training down their throat. Tie their rewards to their performances. Keep them behind the leadership scene, so that they don't rock the boat for you in public. Appreciate them occasionally but not in the presence of your loyal workers, else they will turn around to tell everyone that they are your special people and the brain behind your successes. Their statements stir up calm waters. Some desperate workforces can be very loyal, just like Elisha who went after Elijah to receive the mantle of authority. His desperate nature was seen when he demanded a double portion of the power in Elijah.

- Coping with a non-desperate workforce: These people like

sitting on the fence in most cases and may not be ready to yield their efforts to drive the vision with you. They must be convinced all the time that the vision means good for them. Once they can come to terms with your wooing statements, they will buy in and will be working without demanding a reward. Appreciate them in public, and they will work all the more. Invite them to join you in special functions and they will give you their lives. Allow them to represent you on your behalf and they are all yours. Be watchful, they can easily be discouraged and may decide not to work with you any more because they hardly tie any importance to their relationship with you. They don't easily see the bigger picture of whatever they are doing, unlike the desperate types who will want to set up a new establishment with the same objective as yours and may strive hard to get your admirers – congregation or customers. The disciples of Jesus were a non-desperate workforce. They didn't even bother to demand the Holy Spirit, unlike Elisha, who followed Elijah to receive the power that would announce him.

2. Defining obligations

Our obligations are seen in where our authority lies. This explains our responsibilities and loyalty. A clearly defined obligation helps the leader to measure his performance. In some cases, the obligations may not be clearly defined, and the leader has to discover them by fits and starts. A successful leader is one who knows his obligations ahead of time, and works hard to sustain them as he progresses in his vision drive. Checks and balances are inserted at defined bridge crossings. This helps the leader to take proactive or reactive decisions. A leader should also, during the monitoring process, define the obligations of those he leads, ensuring that they are fully empowered and that they take full ownership of whatever are their duties. There must be a constitution in place that defines everyone's responsibilities, office tenure and office candidacy qualifications.

3. Enforcing leadership presence

Your presence is important to the success of your vision. The people you lead want to hear your voice and footsteps behind and your picture ahead of them. That is what represents the vision you are driving in their mind. You must be able to fill their thoughts with your wise sayings through repetitive teaching. You must be ready to carry the weak along, render help to one who is discouraged about life and also be a relative to those who have none.

One easy way to know that you are present in the hearts of the led is how they respond to your instructions. When they are defiant, you may need to woo them more or become more attached to the few that support you, else you are on your way to downfall. Check how they respond to sharing flyers carrying your picture. If they find it difficult to advertise the vision you stand for in the public, they can't work with you. Jesus taught us that those who deny Him in public He will also deny before God. Those who are not ready to carry their cross and follow Him are not worthy of Him. A look at 2 Kings 18:36 will explain this better: 'But the people held their peace and answered him not a word; for the king's commandment was, 'Do not answer him'.' This is how you know that your presence as their leader is live in their hearts. The story that led to the quoted verse above had it that the king of Assyria sent his men to go and mock King Hezekiah. The people had seen that Hezekiah had given to the king of Assyria all the treasures of the house of the Lord, which shows defeat literally, but they were still ready to obey Hezekiah. This is leadership presence. Those you lead are ready to stand by you to the end if they see their day-by-day living in you.

4. Dealing with rebels

God hates rebellious people. Rebellion is a vision destroyer. The children of Israel perambulated in the wilderness for 40 years instead of 40 days. A total of 39 years, 10 months and about 20 days was wasted as a result of their rebellious acts in the wilderness, costing them their lives and the regard God had for them. This is what rebellion does to any vision. Jesus sent Judas out when it was time to have the last supper with His disciples. Moses cursed them to perish in an earthquake. Miriam, his own sister, was struck with leprosy by God. We all know how God dealt with rebels – they should be shown the way out. Rebellious people are mockers. They are out to oust you out of office. You must watch for rebellious characters among those you lead and set them as public examples by revealing their ugly act and how it is affecting the growth of the vision in terms of reputation and finances. People understand implications when they are tied to money. Let everyone know how their rebellious attitude of gossip and mockery has made it difficult for the vision to yield fruits that would have lifted everyone higher than they are now. This, well said, can go a long way to revive your failing ends and strengthening the loyal members among your team.

CHAPTER
TWENTY TWO

LEADERSHIP BARRIERS

Every leadership is faced with barriers that tend to hinder the vision of the leader. These barriers, if successfully harnessed, could bring out the best in the leader as he strives to develop himself in wisdom, knowledge and understanding to overcome the threats he sees. If, however, they are not harnessed adequately, they have the potential of thwarting his efforts. Some of these are explained below:

- Socio-cultural belief: We have all lived our lives within the tenets of different cultures. Many of us, even as we have received western education, still show strong affinity and adherence to these cultures, which now forms the foundation of whatever we think and do. For instance, the Yoruba ethnic group in Nigeria fall prostrate in respect to their elders. This implies that an elderly subordinate who has a younger leader or a female as his head may find it difficult to exercise himself.

If a young leader or a woman wants the loyalty of an elderly subordinate from such a tribe, what will he do?

There are people who have grown up in cultures where the younger ones bear the luggage of the elderly. If the younger is the leader, what will the elderly from such a background do? This is where wisdom and the upbringing of the leader come to play.

• Age difference barrier: There is often restraint on the part of a leader who has those older than himself in his team. In most cases, the elderly want him to rely on them for opinions on how he should lead. This was the problem with Aaron and Miriam as they questioned Moses' superiority over their ability in leadership (Numbers 12).

• Gender barrier: Many don't respect women leaders – they are seen to be too hard to please. Special legislation against gender inequality must be in place to prevent anarchy. This has been widely defined as diversity and inclusiveness, though this term includes cultures and languages also. If God accepted Deborah as a judge in Israel, there should be no gender barrier in our leadership institutions.

• Prior experience barrier: Many of those we are leading might have prior experience from those they had submitted to earlier and their principles are varied – how do you cope with them? This can be inferred from Jesus' statement in Luke 5:39: 'No man also having drunk old wine straightway desireth new: for he saith, The old is better.' If well managed this could actually lead to improvement, especially when the knowledge already gained is relevant to what is needed. The leader who oversees such people needs to do more on indoctrination and programmed training.

• Media influence: The power of the media cannot be over-emphasized. Closely related to this is how NGOs and pressure groups use the media against leaders, sometime positively and sometime negatively, as a means of pressing home their demands and gaining public opinion in their favour. How are you going to cope if your vision is being attacked by the media and pressure groups? This is why we need to ensure integrity safety at all time.

• Professional barrier: Though leaders don't have a specified form of training, our individual professions have a way of affecting our performance as leaders. For instance the difference between an engineering leader and an accountant as a leader would be in how they make investment decisions. While the engineer sees the finished product's quality and aesthetics as motivation, the accountant may be more concerned about value for money. Every leader who is foreseeing progress should have wide knowledge of professions and careers, though he may not be an expert in them. This will help him to become more relevant to these professionals as he is able to speak in their languages when the need arises. Jesus did this often as He explained His parables using different professional terms. Once those you lead can hear you in their own languages, which was why the disciples were given the gifts of tongues in Acts 2, they will see you as one of their own and would be willing to release the secrets in their hearts for you, in order to enable you to succeed from their own angle.

• Financial barrier: The Bible says 'money answereth all things' – Ecclesiastes 10:19. Many leaders' visions have been locked up in their drawers without fruition due to lack of finance. While this may be the case, a leader who is able to sell his vision will definitely receive the patronage of people who will come to ensure that the vision does not grow mucous. This is where the anointing of the Lord comes in. Whatever the Lord touches will see increase because He is increase Himself. Those who have the money want to see a dedicated leader before they can release their hard-earned money to support him. A leader who is driving a vision should not start from the outset to look for financial donors. Start with what you have, people will see the progress you are making and they will join to support you.

Every leader must start from small beginnings using personal funds to drive the vision. This period of sacrifice is when the leader knows what prudence is all about and will use this principle later to enlighten those who will work with you. The Bible also says the leader will have enough finance to support him from the Gentile nations in Isaiah 61:6-7: 'But ye shall be named the Priests of the Lord: men shall call you the Ministers of our God: ye shall eat the riches of the Gentiles, and in their glory shall ye boast yourselves. For your shame ye shall have double; and for confusion they shall rejoice in their portion: therefore in their land they shall possess the double: everlasting joy shall be unto them.'

The requirement to enjoy this benefit by inference from the portion we just read is when you are a serving leader - men shall call you the Ministers of our God. There is a period of shame, confusion and joy, as seen in verse 7. People will mock you at the outset, making you feel ashamed. I was mocked by many who even said to my face that I started a church to make money. I became more confused by the day when men deserted me. The joy I see today is as a result of my dependence on the promises of the Lord (Psalm 40:1), who speaks to me from behind – Isaiah 30:21: 'And thine ears shall hear a word behind thee, saying, This is the way, walk ye in it, when ye turn to the right hand, and when ye turn to the left'.

• Political barrier: The politics in an environment often affects how a leader takes decisions. Business successes, even the survival of churches, depend on the politics that exist in an environment. For instance, starting a church in the northern part of Nigeria and many Muslim nations is a difficult task. The leader operating in an unfavourable environment must be ready to face opposition and must also have the heart to accept hoodlums destroying their properties when it does happen. Many people also find it difficult to operate in a military leadership environment.

• Wisdom barrier: In Jeremiah 8:9 the Lord made it clear that those who don't have His wisdom will definitely be ashamed. Running your vision based on worldly wisdom will only bring failure. There are many leaders who don't seek after wisdom but rely solely on what the academic books have to offer. Over years leaders of nations have relied on academic economic principles to manage the economy and as they do, they also discover that they don't have answers to all the economic issues that arise. Adam lost his empire because of lack of wisdom from God to handle the situation when needed. Wisdom breeds knowledge and understanding. The reliance on the wisdom of God will help any leader to succeed.

• Language barrier: This is the reason why many organisations encourage the use of a common language in their communications. People are isolated from one another when they are unable to understand each other due to differences in language. This is why God says He will give his children a pure language, in Zephaniah 3:9: 'For then will I turn to the people a pure language, that they may all call upon the name of the Lord, to serve him with one consent'. We can also see that the moment God gave the people of the world different languages during the building of the tower of Babel, that vision was neglected – Genesis 11:6-8: 'And the Lord said, Behold, the people is one, and they have all one language; and this they begin to do: and now nothing will be restrained from them, which they have imagined to do. Go to, let us go down, and there confound their language, that they may not understand one another's speech. So the Lord scattered them abroad from thence upon the face of all the earth: and they left off to build the city'.

Language barriers can lead to the early extermination of your vision, as we can see above. Encourage the use of a common lingua-franca so that people won't start to have sectional leaders, resulting in pressure groups within your organisation. Apart from the language we speak, we could also see the effect of a language barrier as meaning people have different goals to drive within your organisation instead of the common goal that defines the vision you are driving. Naturally this is what is obtainable, but as a leader, your ability to manage these individual aspirations and ensure that they focus on the objective of the vision you drive explains how far you will go in this leadership drive.

CHAPTER TWENTY THREE

LEADERSHIP DELEGATION

Delegation is the act of handing over some of your responsibilities to your associates, subordinates, followers etc, in order to give them an opportunity to learn and grow in management affairs. I have classified leadership delegation as both productive and non-productive. A productive leadership delegation is one which yields results geared towards actualizing the goals of the vision, while a non-productive delegation is often the outcome of non-performance by those authority has been delegated to.

Delegation gives birth to succession, implying that for there to be effective vision-driven leadership succession, there must have been a series of successful vision-driven productive delegations in place. Even within the productive delegation, I have seen that we could actually say that we also have objective – goal-driven and leadership-oriented, and subjective – bias and non-leadership oriented - productive delegation, depending on the leadership ideals.

How then, can a leader delegate successfully? This will become obvious as we discuss further.

Our example will also come from the Bible. Jesus delegated to His disciples on some occasions – they went out to preach the gospel (Matthew 10:7) and they also baptised (John 4:2). A time came when they were unable to cast out demons (Matthew 17:19), but they at least attempted to. This is how delegation works.

1. Productive leadership delegation:

This is a result-oriented delegation. The terms are clearly stated and the delegate knows exactly what he/she will achieve at the end of the day. I have classified this into objective and subjective productive leadership delegation.

- Objective productive leadership delegation: This type of delegation focuses on goals and how best to achieve them. It is my favoured pattern of delegation, because it makes maximum use of people's strength and giving them the opportunity to contribute maximally to the vision the leader is driving. In this kind of delegation, the leader looks out for eye-servicers and takes them through a training process that will make them yield their strength

195

for the work. The leader discourages gossip and favouritism among the workforce, because he is in search of a vision-driven productive successor. Jesus turned down James' and John's mother's request to favour her sons. This is the beauty of an objective productive leadership. If our leadership institutions employ the services of only those who meant well for the vision they drive, leaders will be available who will sustain the growth and effectiveness of our visions of sustainability.

- Subjective productive leadership delegation: Leaders often delegate responsibilities to those who eye-service them, not on the fact that these subordinates are result driven, but just to ensure that they keep on receiving praise and respect from such staff. In such instances, depending on the tasks assigned to such a staff, the onus of performance measurement rests on the bond of relationship existing between them. Once they break out, the performance of the staff will automatically dwindle as the superior now rates him/her as a low performer. Everything done here, though productive in sense, is filled with bias. When a member of staff who gets delegation through this means assumes a higher leadership position via succession, such an establishment will experience anarchy, because he/she will be looking for those who will take over his duties while he answers the boss's name, taking all the glory for free.

CHAPTER TWENTY THREE

2. Non-Productive Leadership Delegation:

When we delegate authority to serve into the hands of a novice, then we are sure of non-productivity. The Bible taught us this when it says: 'As for my people, children are their oppressors, and women rule over them. O my people, they which lead thee cause thee to err, and destroy the way of thy paths.' – Isaiah 3:12, 'Woe to thee, O land, when thy king is a child' – Ecclesiastes 10:16

What is referred to in the verses we just read is leadership incompetence (woman), and immaturity (child) (Galatians 4:1-2). It does not mean in context that women cannot rule effectively or that the young cannot lead. Indeed Deborah was Israel's judge at a time (Judges 4:4) and she was successful, and at the age of twenty five years Hezekiah was already a king in Judah (2 Chronicles 29:1), and he pleased God.

Non-productive delegation causes chaos in an organisation. Incompetence and immaturity may be overcome through training – formal and on-the job - and mentoring. The inability of Jesus disciples to heal the boy suffering from epilepsy shows this, but when they asked, Jesus did teach them what they needed to be able to carry out such deliverance.

Even the Lord's Prayer shows that the disciples have been having non-productive prayers and they were desirous to be taught by Jesus as they saw the results Jesus' prayers were producing. After Jesus' resurrection we would see how He continually taught them before His ascension, and finally He released the Holy Spirit to them and they became productive, carrying out the vision of Christ without Jesus' physical supervision.

Leadership delegation is important to the success of leaders in the following ways:

- It enables the leader to assess his leadership influence over those he leads because delegation is always downward, and although it could also be horizontal, while reporting is vertically upward and could also be horizontal. Your leadership influence is hinged on perceived support from those you lead on opinions that originates from you.

- It enables the leader to reduce working stress and increase time spent on rest/leisure because of avoidance of working overtime.

- It enables the leader to spend more quality time with his family as he can now go on leave when due.

- It enables more work to be handled effectively and reduces clumsy targets as the leader now focuses on top management high-end issues.

- It encourages participation of more people in management decision making.

- It coheres team members and allow for issues to be settled at the supervisor level because of their involvement in higher decision-making processes.

- Your subordinates learn and mature quickly in the wisdom and culture of the inherent leadership doctrine within the organisation.

- Since there are more people who can function as high-end leaders as a result of the practice of leadership delegation, there is every tendency that there will be continuity in the event of the absence of the leader.

Since delegation can only thrive in an environment where there is cooperation, the leader must deal with acts of rebellion among his followers or subordinates. Murmuring will only breed discord among your workforce. The earlier this is dealt with, the earlier you will reap the gains of leadership.

The following are guides that will enable you succeed in your leadership delegation:

- Ensure there is an effective line of reporting, so that the idea of favouritism will not be rumoured among your workforce.

- Institute special punishments for unfounded rebellious and murmuring acts.

- Give no room for gender inequality.

- Eliminate fear of failure from the minds of your subordinates through training and overall mental development.

- Delegate only to capable hands, through performance reviews and personal interests of your subordinates, as many may not really be interested in taking up high-end roles and responsibilities.

CHAPTER TWENTY FOUR

LEADERSHIP SUCCESSION

A leader should have a successor who would carry on with his vision. Abraham had Isaac as a successor. Isaac had Jacob as a successor after blessing him. Jacob had the 12 tribes of Israel, whom he blessed, except Ruben, whom he cursed. From the tribe of Levi Moses became a pronounced successor, from where we could say that a leader arises. Moses had Joshua as a successor, whom he actually laid hands on so that he received the spirit of wisdom. Elijah had Elisha.

King Saul couldn't hand over before he died in war due to his heart of jealousy and rejection by God over his sin of disobedience. King David had Solomon to hand over to. Jesus had Peter, whom he publicly judged as the foundation of His church. Saint Peter was the one who spoke publicly in Acts 2 after they were empowered with the Holy Spirit and his shadow indeed healed the sick as a confirmation of him as Christ's successor to lead the others and this was why he was always called upon to minister the Holy Spirit to new converts. Jesus after His resurrection handed over the disciples and the sheep under his care.

Who did St Peter hand over to? We would discover that he even had the occasional fracas with James, who was in Jerusalem and Paul (formerly Saul) over doctrinal issues. Believers are still having disagreements over doctrinal issues. I would say that this is due to Peter's inability to effectively lead the sheep of Christ into doctrinal truths even when they disagreed with him.

Leaders are often faced with the issue of having a successor. We would see that St Paul had to decry Demas' attitude towards the gospel and asked for Mark to come and support him (2 Timothy 4:10-11). His relationship with Timothy would be seen as that of a leader happy to have found someone who will carry on with the vision he preached.

The process of scouting for a successor has to be done spiritually and physically. In this world, especially where we have the monarchical form of leadership, the heir to the throne is usually the first son, and he is attached to those who will train him on kingship affairs and the history of his people. The process is often termed indoctrination and enculturation. Even in the family front, especially in Africa, the first son is seen as a successor to the father.

The fear of every serving leader is how he can institute a

successor who will take over from him. In the following discussion we will see how this may be done.

- Pray for God to give you a successor: This is the most effective way. Moses asked God to tell him those who would work with him (Exodus 33:12). The prayer of Jesus in John 17 confirmed that only God can give you a successor. This process should be started as early as possible. Jesus had his successor in the midst of His disciples who started with Him. This is why a leader is not always happy when those he hoped to succeed him eventually depart for their own vision, as happened between Demas and Paul. This is the trend in most churches worldwide, and this disagreement usually comes through the wife of the supposed succeeding leader over the issue of money.

- Indoctrinate the successor once you have found one: Indoctrination is a planned teaching and walking process. The declaration of Peter about who Christ was shows that he was indeed getting indoctrinated faster. You should also let him know the obstacles that he may face ahead, as Jesus did when he told Peter in John 21:18: 'Verily, verily, I say unto thee, When thou wast young, thou girdest thyself, and walkedst whither thou wouldest: but when thou shalt be old, thou shalt stretch forth thy hands, and another shall gird thee, and carry thee whither thou wouldest not.'

The training package should be robust enough to help him mature on time, with vision and purpose live in his heart. Successors should be ready to be as their master, whom they are learning from. St Paul says in Philippians 4:9: 'The things which you learned and received and heard and saw in me, these do, and the God of peace will be with you'. Earlier in Philippians 4:8, he revealed that the only way to receive the gift of virtue that will lead to joy in the heart of the successor, which he referred to as, 'anything praiseworthy,' is by meditation. This could be said to mean his personal relationship with God.

- Give him the opportunity to lead while you are there. Joshua was among those spies who were sent to spy the land of Canaan, and he was among those who brought good tidings from the land. Jesus gave the opportunity for his disciples to do what they saw him do.

- Appraise his performance periodically: Periodic appraisal teaches you what character to reinforce and what to change. It also creates an avenue for continual discussion to know how the prodigy is faring, the challenges he may be experiencing and his desires. Appraisals help you to nip in the bud any early attitudes of discouragement.

- Encourage a positive attitude. When you encourage positive attitudes, you reinforce such attitudes in him. This sings a song of motivation in his heart, and also tells him that the act of leadership is not as frightening as he might have thought. In the beginning of Jesus' ministry, Peter confessed that he wasn't worthy to walk with Jesus. As they walked together, Christ's approval of him made him ready to take up the mantle even while he felt angry with the view that Christ didn't trust his ability to lead (John 21:15-17).

- Correct any anomaly you see in his leadership call: It is your duty to correct any act of irregularity you discover in your successor as it relates to the vision he is bearing. Jesus once rebuked Peter publicly. Then when they were on shore with him after His resurrection, the act of abandonment of duty, as Peter took the rest to fish at sea instead of the gospel was corrected, John 21.

- Document who your successor would be: This is necessary in the event of an accident. Moses had laid hands on Joshua before he died. David had been anointed before Saul died. In the event that you were unable to appoint a successor, this document will be a guide. This, if prayerfully done, will ensure that the next successor will be someone who will lead as God wants.

- Successor by credentials or vote: This seldom happens as a means of selecting a successor. However what has happened over time is that such successors often come in to drive their own vision and projects, leading to underdevelopment in areas that don't catch their fancy, or if he had trouble with his predecessor as always happens in political governance. This is like a fallback plan when there is no formal appointment of a successor by the outgoing leader, or when there is documentation that denies the outgoing leader the opportunity to appoint a successor. It is my candid advice that the outgoing leader must have a say in who becomes his successor for the purpose of vision continuity, except in cases when it is judged that the outgoing leader does not possess the qualities that would enable him to make the right choice, especially for corrupt leaders.

CHAPTER TWENTY FIVE

LEADERSHIP PROSPERITY

A prospering leader is the one who has the fear of God in his heart. The book of 2 Chronicles 31:20-21 says: 'Thus Hezekiah did throughout all Judah, and he did what was good and right and true before the Lord his God. And in every work that he began in the service of the house of God, in the law and in the commandment, to seek his God, he did it with all his heart. So he prospered'.

The reason why he prospered is the underlying fact we are discussing in this chapter. He did all that he did with his heart, and the Bible says, 'So he prospered.' Leadership prosperity is all about obeying God in all that we do as leaders so as to bring joy and peace into the lives of those we lead. There is always a point of announcement that leads to a higher calling and benefit. This the Bible preaches too: 'From the end of the earth will I cry unto thee, when my heart is overwhelmed: lead me to the rock that is higher than I.' –

Psalms 61:2. The Psalmist says that God should lead him to the rock that is higher than him – a rock that represents leadership prosperity, because his heart is plagued by disappointments.

A leader who wants those he leads to prosper must be ready to encourage the people to make provisions for the service of God, and this he must do through leading by example. When the Lord blesses the people and they give their offerings into the house of the Lord so that those who officiate therein will have enough to eat, intercede on their behalf, and also be able to teach them the word of the Lord, the land will experience abundance. This also applies to business outfits. When the employees don't deny God their resources, the company will see increase. A church where the leaders eat their tithes will also find it difficult to experience the increase of the Lord.

The Bible says in 2 Chronicles 31:10: 'And Azariah the chief priest, from the house of Zadok, answered him and said, 'Since the people began to bring the offerings into the house of the Lord, we have had enough to eat and have plenty left, for the Lord has blessed His people; and what is left is this great abundance.' God blessed the people because they had a leader whose heart loved God and was dedicated to the instructions of God.

Now we can explain what leadership prosperity entails below:

- The people you are leading rejoice, because they experience peace and a cordial relationship with God, their creator.

- They have enough to eat and to bring to the house of the Lord. There is no starvation in the land. Progress in seen at every quarter and not for those in leadership only.

- There is unity of purpose among those you lead as they obey every instruction you give them in furtherance of the vision you are driving.

- They have basic social amenities. We saw that Hezekiah provided water for his people in 2 Chronicles 32:30. Those you lead must have access to basic amenities of life. This is what makes you a leader who acts with the heart of God. We all know that God provides light, water and shelter (caves) for us. He also made available His word for us to gain knowledge and understanding through His shepherds, and good fruits for good health. Every leader with the fear of God at heart must be ready to provide those he leads with these amenities: electricity, good water, shelter, education and good health care.

- The leader too would prosper in wealth and riches, but not by robbing those he leads. The story of Hezekiah had it that God made him prosperous in material wealth: 'Moreover he provided cities for himself, and possessions of flocks and herds in abundance; for God had given him very much wealth' – 2 Chronicles 32:29. This implies that a leader who fears God and does His command will certainly experience God's blessings. But we must be ready to seek the kingdom of God and His righteousness first, Matthew 6:33.

The Bible says that God is happy when the righteous prosper in all that they do: 'Let the Lord be magnified, which hath pleasure in the prosperity of his servant'. - Psalm 35:27. How then can leaders sustain all-round prosperity as they lead? This is what we will discuss below:

- The leader must recognise that they are only given an opportunity to lead God's children and as such they must be ready to focus their attention on God, who will provide all their needs through Jesus Christ. This will ensure the presence of both spiritual and physical prosperity in their lives in line with Saint John's wish in 3 John 3:2: 'Beloved, I pray that you may prosper in all things and be in good health, just as your soul prospers'.

- The leader must be ready to be submissive to God in thoughts and deeds so as to maintain a cordial and a spiritual relationship with God. This way, enemies will find it difficult to break into his territory to destabilise the peace around him. This was what happened to Solomon after he submitted to the wisdom of God in his leadership striving until he was led astray. He indeed confessed that God gave him peace. There is no peace without prosperity. It is a clear Biblical fact that King Solomon was prosperous. The secret was the peace he experienced that made him prosper as he confessed in 1 Kings 5:4: 'But now the Lord my God has given me rest on every side; there is neither adversary nor evil occurrence'.

- He must institute a worship order in line with the Bible to encourage those he leads to have a time of fellowship with their God, as we read earlier about the acts of King Hezekiah in 2 Chronicles 29. There are many bosses in the office who would not give a damn for their employees' request to go to church services after close of work, as these bosses often work late. In such circumstances, the leader will begin to reap ill will in his staff, distrust, stealing, lies, etc, because they no longer fear God. A leader could even encourage those he leads to seek the face of God concerning a decision he is about to make.

- In all, leadership prosperity comes through the fear of God, sacrifice, prudence, accountability and diligence in service. These must be encouraged by the leader, who must lead by example in these spheres of leadership.

CHAPTER
TWENTY SIX

HELP FOR FAILING LEADERS

Leaders begin to experience failure when they are unable to live their vision. As we have said, leadership is about problem solving and removing stumbling-blocks out of the way of the children of God so that they will inherit their blessings through equipping them with the knowledge to succeed (Isaiah 57:14). The first step in helping a leader who is failing is to re-image him to God, so that he/she can start seeing his/her duty in the circle of God, or in the kingdom of God.

Jesus did this when He sent His disciples to the lost sheep of Israel (Matthew 10:6). The book of Nahum 1:7 says: 'The Lord is good, A stronghold in the day of trouble; And He knows those who trust in Him'. This verse is the assurance every failing leader needs to know to get out of trouble. A look into the Bible will show that it is only when God is against leaders that they experience failure. Also in the book of Nahum 3:5 we would see what the word of the Lord says: 'Behold, I am against you' says the Lord of hosts.

What happened as a result of this hatred from God? The end of that verse explains the result of this proclamation from God: 'I will lift your skirts over your face, I will show the nations your nakedness, And the kingdoms your shame'. The last line talks about the kingdoms, meaning that God was speaking to a people under a leadership that was failing. The outcome of having a leader rejected by God is not worth accepting, because those he leads will definitely not experience peace, progress and unity. This is all the more reason a failing leader needs to be helped by all through prayers and our public complaints so that he would repent. If we sit on the fence while we allow him to lead as he likes, we and our children, including generations unborn, will experience bitterness.

Verse 1 of Nahum chapter 3 says: 'Woe to the bloody city! It is all full of lies and robbery'. One would say that the situation referred to here could be well described as a state of anarchy. What was the leader doing to the extent that his kingdom would become a den for all manner of evil doers? As leaders, we should ask ourselves such questions relating to the level of peace, progress and unity in our homes and wherever our leadership disposition is needed. We shouldn't wait until we have the situation decried in the book of Nahum before we start seeking for help. This is why we discussed progress review earlier on. A leader who puts his leadership under checks and balances will never go astray. Once a leader goes astray, neglecting God as he carries out his leadership duties, he will certainly be rejected by God. A rejected leader is a time bomb waiting to explode and cause destruction to lives and properties.

In industry there are work areas called 'confined spaces', and the safety rules state that a special procedure has to be developed and approved according to industry standards by respected authorities, and then a special work permit must be obtained before one enters into a confined space. A confined space is a potential death trap for anyone who enters there, because of the possibility of not having enough life-supporting oxygen. A failing leader is like someone in a confined space. Such a leader has no visible life in them and anyone they call to themselves and lead is heading for death.

We must see the call to help failing leaders as a passionate desire for excellent leadership in all spheres of human endeavour. The Bible says in Isaiah 56:9-10: 'All ye beasts of the field, come to devour, yea, all ye beasts in the forest. His watchmen are blind: they are all ignorant, they are all dumb dogs, they cannot bark; sleeping, lying down, loving to slumber'. In Verse 10 the leaders are called watchmen. These verses explain the fact that when leaders fail to lead successfully, the people are devoured, implying further that there will be untold hardship and agony in the land.

God decried Solomon's negligence of His statute after he

went after foreign gods. God also sent the prophet Nathan to reprimand David over his sin of adultery and murder. Moses failed when he couldn't control his anger. All leaders who are failing need to return to God. The Lord says we must return to Him so that He will become present in our lives, thoughts and actions (Zachariah 1:3, Malachi 3:7).

The evidence of failure is easily seen in poor leadership performance, especially when measured against set standards. Sometime it may have to do with a leader's loyalty to the power that anoints him, or his inability to safeguard his integrity. In the Bible, one sees these as the reasons many failed as leaders. King David had an integrity issue, repented and was given a second chance. King Solomon failed when he compromised both his loyalty to God and integrity. Moses' loyalty to God was compromised when he acted against God's instruction to speak to the rock of Meribah, to bring water to the children of Israel in the wilderness.

There are leadership obligations that guide a leader on his path to success: Authority, Responsibilities and Allegiance. A leader fails when any or all of these leadership obligations are compromised:

1. Authority: The authority you have and how you administer it matters to your ability to sustain your leadership influence.

2. Responsibilities: Those you serve and the overall goal you stand for are your responsibilities. Once there is a hole in your responsibilities to those you lead, society and a compromise on the objective of the vision, you are on your way down.

3. Allegiance: A leader must know who is footing his bills and who he must be loyal to all the time.

For instance, a husband's obligations would be:

- Authority – The head of the family: 'For the husband is the head of the wife, even as Christ is the head of the church: and he is the saviour of the body.' - Ephesians 5:23.

- Responsibilities – husband and father: 'But if any provide not for his own, and especially for those of his own house, he hath denied the faith, and is worse than an infidel. - 1 Timothy 5:8

- Allegiance – Loyalty is to Christ: 'But I would have you know, that the head of every man is Christ; and the head of the woman is the man; and the head of Christ is God.' - 1 Corinthians 11:3.

Let's take a look at the pastor and his obligations:

- Authority – The overseer of the church of Christ: 1 Timothy 3:2-5

- Responsibilities – Feed the church of Christ with knowledge and understanding: 'And I will give you pastors according to mine heart, which shall feed you with knowledge and understanding'. Jeremiah 3:15

- Allegiance – Loyalty is to Christ: 'Christ is the head of the church: and he is the saviour of the body'. Ephesians 5:23.

Leaders need to ascertain daily how they are faring in each of these obligations, else they will fail because they will not keep track of where they are failing. This they can do when they have the fear of God. No one wants to be associated with failure and as such, failing leaders would be seen to have been deserted by those they lead.

The book of Zachariah 8:23 opened my eyes to this fact: 'Thus says the Lord of hosts: 'In those days ten men from every language of the nations shall grasp the sleeve of a Jewish man, saying, 'Let us go with you, for we have heard that God is with you." Once God is with a leader, he does not need to woo people to follow and submit to his leadership vision. This explains why the multitude followed Jesus about even when He lived a simple life in their midst. Many leaders think the only way to make people submit under them is the show of affluence, and as such they want to influence those they lead with the show of wealth as often seen in the political circle.

CHAPTER TWENTY SIX

The Bible says of the reasons why a Bishop may fail in his duty:

1   *This is a true saying, if a man desire the office of a bishop, he desireth a good work.*

2   *A bishop then must be blameless, the husband of one wife, vigilant, sober, of good behaviour, given to hospitality, apt to teach;*

3   *Not given to wine, no striker, not greedy of filthy lucre; but patient, not a brawler, not covetous;*

4   *One that ruleth well his own house, having his children in subjection with all gravity;*

5   *(For if a man know not how to rule his own house, how shall he take care of the church of God?)*

6   *Not a novice, lest being lifted up with pride he fall into the condemnation of the devil.*

7   *Moreover he must have a good report of them which are without; lest he fall into reproach and the snare of the devil. –* 1 Timothy 3:2-7

These statements are typical for every office holder. In verse 1, it was made clear that leadership is about the desire for good works, implying further that any leadership that is devoid of good works will not succeed. Verse 2 talks about the quality of one who has the fear of God at heart. Is there any leader who will succeed without having God by him? This is why

Christ says we must be as perfect as God in thoughts and reasoning, Matthew 5:48.

A look into the other verses above would explain to us what we need to become effective leaders. Verse 6 says that the leader must not be a novice. This is why we discussed leadership knowledge earlier. A leader who is failing in his duties needs to be empowered with knowledge through reviving his relationship with God, attending leadership seminars, conferences and workshops.

Moses spent time with God often, as he encountered problems leading the children of Israel. You must spend time with God, who made all things, so that your leadership heart will come alive with the passion and purpose of God. The word of the Lord says in Isaiah 54:17: 'No weapon that is formed against thee shall prosper; and every tongue that shall rise against thee in judgment thou shalt condemn. This is the heritage of the servants of the Lord, and their righteousness is of me, saith the Lord.' Any leader who would submit under the leadership of God will never experience failure because the Lord's guidance is his heritage.

At this juncture, I would want us to summarise the reasons why leaders fail:

1. When they become spiritually blind, ignorant of what is required of them due to the lack of requisite knowledge,

dumb dogs who don't correct wrongs and prevent the intrusion of deceptive knowledge into the heart of those they lead, sleeping instead of being active, lying down when they are suppose to be watchful through prayers and seeking the face of God, and when they slumber – Isaiah 56:10: 'His watchmen are blind: they are all ignorant, they are all dumb dogs, they cannot bark; sleeping, lying down, loving to slumber.'

2. When they are greedy, leading for selfish gains, lack deep understanding of spiritual things, and fight to defend their wealth – Isaiah 56:11: 'Yea, they are greedy dogs which can never have enough, and they are shepherds that cannot understand: they all look to their own way, every one for his gain, from his quarter'.

3. When they drink hot drinks and feed those they lead with same in order to avert justice, as those that drink with them will find nothing wrong with what they do, while they leave the weightier matters of leadership in favour of non-profit-making investments that will only enrich them the more. King Lemuel's mother advised him against alcoholic drink in Proverbs 31:4-5: 'It is not for kings, O Lemuel, it is not for kings to drink wine; nor for princes strong drink: Lest they drink, and forget the law, and pervert the judgment of any of the afflicted'.

One of the easiest ways to know a leader who will not succeed is his appetite for drinks and unnecessary celebrations. I have seen over time that most celebrated leaders while they are serving often become failing leaders. This is because their acts of 'dancing to the gallery' are actually the reason behind their popularity. They have flattering tongues aimed at deceiving those they lead and rendering them helpless. This is well captured in Isaiah 56:12: 'Come ye, say they, I will fetch wine, and we will fill ourselves with strong drink; and tomorrow shall be as this day, and much more abundant.'

4. When they cannot stand to defend those who meant good for the success and progress of their vision but will rather accept lies from their subordinates, who try to undo the innocent and morally upright ones among them. A leader who cannot stand for integrity and uprightness will never see increase – Isaiah 57:1: 'The righteous perisheth, and no man layeth it to heart: and merciful men are taken away, none considering that the righteous is taken away from the evil to come'. The more this happens the more your vision will experience bankruptcy. It is often said that good people don't last long, not only in life, but wherever they function as leaders or subordinates, because of the devices of the enemy. Every leader should watch out for those who eye-service them and those who often say they do everything

in their establishments without referring to the achievement as a team effort.

5. When they have poor upbringing. The first education we usually live with is the one we had from our parents. The children of sorcerers, witch doctors and idolaters alike, the children of adulterers – King Solomon is an example of a king from such a background - and the children of whores – Jephthah, whose mother was a harlot, made unreasonable vows - who finally become leaders have their leadership ideals often polluted except the Lord lives in their hearts – Isaiah 57:3-5: 'But draw near hither, ye sons of the sorceress, the seed of the adulterer and the whore. Against whom do ye sport yourselves? Against whom make ye a wide mouth, and draw out the tongue? are ye not children of transgression, a seed of falsehood. Enflaming yourselves with idols under every green tree, slaying the children in the valleys under the clefts of the rocks?'

Not until these sets of leaders come to God and repent of their ways will they see success in their bids for leadership. No nation which has an idolatrous leader will experience peace and progress. This is the fate of most nations worldwide.

* * * * *

Take what we have discussed above to hear, to learn to do well all the time. You will only succeed as a leader when the Lord is with you. I see you succeeding in your leadership campaign as you yield to the lead of God from today henceforth. Amen!

God bless you.

BOOKS BY THE SAME AUTHOR

Existing In The Supernatural

The Altar In Golgotha

How Good and Large is your Land?

Born To Blossom

Battles Beyond The Physical

The Path To Absolute Freedom

The Man God Made

Aspects of Marriage

Leadership – An Eagle Eye Perspective

To contact Pastor Oghenethoja Umuteme send an email to
president@christmovementinternational.org
You can join him on Facebook and Twitter also:
www.facebook.com/Pst Oghenethoja Umuteme
www.twitter.com/PstUmuteme
WORSHIP WITH US
@
ROYAL DIAMONDS INTERNATIONAL CHURCH
(aka Christ Movement)
Nnata Close by Weli Street
Rumunduru/Eneka Road
Rumunduru
Port Harcourt, Nigeria
Please call or send us email to know our worship days and time.
Phone: +234-8086737791
Email: christmovementinternational@gmail.com
info@christmovementinternational.org

2374093R00128

Printed in Great Britain
by Amazon.co.uk, Ltd.,
Marston Gate.